Horses of the Light
The Outback Riders - 2

LEANNE OWENS

Copyright © 2019 Leanne Owens
eBook published 2012
Cover photo and art by Kate Owens
All rights reserved.
ISBN: 978-16-91106-25-7

DEDICATION

For you, dear reader. Whoever you are, wherever and whenever – dream big, plan well, work hard, and achieve the amazing. It's never too early to start, and it's never too late. Remember, your greatness doesn't lie in your wealth or your power; it lies in your kindness to others and the world around you. So, read on about a group of outback riders who dream, plan, and work to make their dreams happen.

CONTENTS

1	Find the Min Min	1
2	Home Again	17
3	Going Camping	35
4	The Cry of the Min Min	51
5	The Galaxy Walk	69
6	The Calm Before the Storm	89
7	Amy and Brandon 1.30 pm – 2.45 pm	107
8	Jake, Meat, and Skinner 2 pm – 3.05 pm	113
9	Dane, Lani, and Matthew 2.30 pm – 3.10 pm	121
10	Amy and Brandon 2.45 pm – 3.40 pm	127
11	Dane, Lani, and Matthew 3.10 pm – 4 pm	145
12	Amy and Brandon 4 pm – 7 pm	165
13	Sundown	175
14	The Arrival of the Min Min	191
15	Keeping Secrets	207
16	Jake and Meat	227
17	Christmas	229

CHAPTER ONE
Find the Min Min

'So, what are we going to do these holidays?' Lani asked, leaning over the back of the seat to talk to her brother, Dane. He lounged across two seats as their bus pulled out of the Brisbane Transit Centre to begin the eighteen-hour journey to Longreach in outback Queensland.

It was the end of the school year, and students who had been away at boarding school in the cities were climbing into buses, planes, and cars to head home to their remote properties for seven weeks of summer holidays. Dane Winter, at fourteen, had just completed Year Nine, and his sister, Lani, and cousin, Amy King, both a year younger, finished Year Eight.

'Nothing,' Dane yawned and stretched his legs out into the aisle. 'Abso-blinking-lutely nothing.'

'I'm going to start riding Laddie,' said Amy, kneeling on the bus seat next to Lani so she could talk to Dane. 'We have a lot of training to do together. Groundwork, groundwork, groundwork.'

'Boring, boring, boring,' Dane rolled his eyes and ducked out of the way of her half-hearted punch. 'It's the summer holidays – you can't get too serious about training your horse the whole time.'

'Not every minute of it,' Amy grimaced at him. 'I'm also going to sleep, eat, and swim occasionally. I want to spend a fair bit of time getting the basics right with him.'

Dane rolled his eyes at her and ducked again as she leaned over to swat at him.

'Don't make fun of me, Dane,' she warned him.

'I'm not making fun of you,' he grinned, 'I'm making fun of your boring plans. We have seven weeks ahead of us. It's summer. We need something big and memorable, not an entire holiday of teaching the basics to your horse.'

'It hurts to admit it,' Lani sighed, sinking back into her seat so that she faced the front of the bus, 'but he has a point. This is your first Christmas with us. We need to make it unforgettable in case it's the only Christmas you have at Sunhaven.'

'If it's my only Christmas with you,' Amy pointed out as she slid around to sit next to Lani, 'it's going to be unforgettable, no matter what we do.'

'Yeah, but it should be something special,' said Lani, thinking hard. 'Like head up to Muttaburra and take kayaks down the Thompson River and then the Cooper, and see how far we can go in a week. Or ride to Longreach on the horses.'

'The rivers are too dangerous in the wet season,' Dane stuck his head over the back of their seats and spoke down to them, dismissing his sister's suggestions, 'and it's too hot to ride to Longreach.'

'Then, how about we go and see the dinosaur tracks over at Lark Quarry. Amy hasn't seen them yet.'

'Oh yeah, great idea,' Dane's voice dripped with sarcasm. 'We're trying to fill up fifty days, and that will take up all of one of them.'

'Then you come up with something,' Lani bristled, looking up at him, 'but make it good. When Amy's parents come back from overseas, I want her to remember this as the best Christmas ever.'

'It will be,' Amy promised her.

She smiled at Lani, thinking how much she liked her cousins when less than six months ago she had never met them and didn't even know their names; they were just the family her mother occasionally mentioned as living in the wilds of Queensland. Their mothers were sisters who had never been close, so it had been a shock to Amy when her mother and step-father went overseas to work and left her with a family she didn't know.

She had been part of their family since the September holidays when she moved there against her will. There was a vast cultural difference between living near the densely populated city of Melbourne in Victoria and the vast open plains of outback Queensland. At first, Amy had been determined to dislike the Winter family and had done everything possible to convince them she should return to live with friends in Victoria.

Her desire to leave evaporated the night tragedy struck the Winter family. Her Uncle Geoff died in a car accident on the station, and Amy had ridden for help in a storm. Until the moment she vaulted her uncle's horse, her cousins had no idea that their Amy King was Amity Fielding-King, one of the leading young event riders in the country.

With no communications because of damage by the storm and no way to get a vehicle out for help, Amy had crossed the Sunhaven Hills, jumping Laddie over Legend's Leap, the narrow point of the gorge with a four-meter gap and a fifty-meter drop below. The Min Min lights helped guide her in the darkness to Brindella Fells Station, where she could organize help.

After Geoff Winter's funeral, the family tried to pick up their lives, as they knew Geoff wanted them to continue with Sunhaven. They surprised Amy by buying back her two competition horses and gave her Laddie, Uncle Geoff's horse because they knew he was Amy's dream eventing horse.

For Amy, Christmas was usually a quiet time as her parents didn't value traditions, and her friends went away on holidays, so she just spent the days with her horses. Her father died in South America five years earlier, so Christmas Day was spent with her mother and step-father. They were more dedicated to their work as archaeologists than to the notion of giving their daughter a memorable Christmas.

Twice her mother had shifted their Christmas celebrations to another day that was more convenient for her work commitments. Amy recalled sitting alone in their house watching Christmas specials on television, wishing the spirit of the season would touch her mother. It didn't. Amy had longed for a real Christmas surrounded by family and goodwill rather than a hurried affair that needed to fit between writing an article and preparing for another archaeological dig. To her mother, Christmas was no more important than an annual dental check-up which was moved around to suit other appointments.

This year, spending the festivities with her aunt, her three cousins, and their Uncle John on Sunhaven Station was going to be the best Christmas ever. Lani had described the setting up of the Christmas tree, the massive pile of presents under the tree, the visits from friends and neighbors, and the general feel of the time of celebration. It sounded like everything Amy had always dreamed it could be in a family that valued Christmas.

'Believe me, it'll be the best Christmas ever,' Amy told her. 'Mum never could see why anyone would want to make such a fuss over it all. She thinks Christmas is just a way for retailers to make people spend more money. We never even had a Christmas tree. I used to set a little one up on the desk in my room to make it feel a bit special. Mum would complain about me running up the electricity bill because I put some fairy lights up in my window.'

'That's sad,' Lani gave her a quick hug; she never failed to be surprised at how austere her cousin's life had been. 'Our Christmas will make up for it. We have great Christmas times, with carols and parties. Santa turns up for all the little kids at the parties. Friends fly in to visit. It's just the best.'

'I've got it!' exclaimed Dane, almost leaping over the seat to join them in his moment of revelation, not caring that he was interrupting his sister. 'I know what we can do to make these holidays awesome.'

The excitement in his voice convinced the girls that he had thought of something and wasn't going to give them one of his lame plans that would leave them groaning at his humor. Sometimes, what his teenage-boy-brain saw as amusing had them shaking their heads in pity for his slow development in that area.

'The lights.' He grinned at them, his brown eyes alight with all the ideas that were running through his mind. 'We'll find the Min Min lights.'

Lani narrowed her eyes at him, giving his suggestion a few seconds of thought as fragments of information relating to the Min Min rushed out of her memory. They were the mysterious lights often sighted in the Winton area for the past few hundred years, and Aboriginal legends spoke of them for far longer than that. They appeared at night, often resembling a set of headlights approaching isolated travelers in the outback, only they kept coming closer and closer, silently, and not following any road. They looked as though they hovered above the ground. They could leap over watchers and move away on the other side, still appearing like headlights facing them, still silent.

The Winter children had grown up with the stories of how the Min Min stole people away or came for their souls when they died. They heard neighbors talk of seeing the lights in the distance, moving across the land in places with no roads, and then vanishing and reappearing somewhere else. Their father had seen them a few times. Uncle John said he'd seen them around Sunhaven Gorge in the hills between their two properties.

On the night that Amy had raced the storm and crossed the Sunhaven Hills to save her family, she had seen them in the gorge. Seconds later, they had appeared among the trees to guide her down the treacherous and winding track to Uncle John's house, a path she'd have never found without their help.

People often spoke of the Min Min lights, but no one knew what they were. Some dismissed them as swamp gas or ball lightning, perhaps lights reflected in a heat haze, or just a figment of the imaginations of lonely travelers. However, once someone had seen them, they knew they were far more than gas, reflected lights, or fantasy. They were an entity of some sort. They helped Amy find her way down a twisting path, so they understood she needed guidance that night.

'Brilliant,' Lani nodded as she weighed up the merits of his plan. 'I love it. I'm surprised, but I love it.'

Amy nodded as well. She wanted to see the lights again.

'We can camp out at the gorge and look for them there,' Dane spoke rapidly as his ideas came tumbling over each other. 'Uncle John reckons they live there, and he's seen them a few times, and Amy saw them that night.' He paused for a moment, remembering that it was the night he watched his father die. It took some effort to shake off the sadness that overcame him when he thought about his father, who had been his hero. Some days, he felt as though there was a blackness creeping towards him. Not today, though, he told himself, forcing away the shadows and imposing a smile over them. 'I say we go looking for them there.'

'And if we find them?' asked Amy, pretending not to notice the bleak look that had clouded Dane's expression. 'It's not like we can go up and ask the Min Min how they are doing, and would they mind telling us what they are. It's not like we're the paparazzi of the Min Min lights.'

Dane and Lani burst into laughter at Amy's words.

'Min Min paparazzi,' chortled Lani. 'That sounds like an outback rap group.'

'But it's not a bad idea,' Dane raised his eyebrows as he thought of something. 'What do the paparazzi always have with them? Cameras. We have to try and get the Min Min on film.'

'We all have cameras,' Lani saw the potential in this idea. 'Our phones have cameras and videos, and Dad had a couple of good video cameras.'

Like her brother, the mention of her father brought a moment of sadness to her. Their mother had explained that this could happen for the rest of their lives. It was essential to acknowledge the grief and loss but keep going. Their father would want them to look forward to all the wonderful times ahead rather than dwell on the sadness of things left behind.

Dane continued, 'We can take the cameras with us and try and get everything on film.'

'We could make a documentary out of it,' put in Amy,

warming to all the possibilities of trying to find the Min Min lights. 'I've made some good short films about my horses, and people thought they looked good. It's easy with the right programs.'

'Good thinking, Ames,' nodded Dane. 'Even if we don't get the Min Min on film, we could make something for YouTube that could get millions of hits – the Outback Riders adventures. It's got to be a winner. Even if our search is a failure, we're sure to get some funny footage of Mathew being an idiot. I've heard of people making big money out of this sort of stuff so, not only will we have something totally awesome to do during the holidays, but we'll also make money out of it.'

'We need to start writing things down,' said Lani as she rifled through her bag, looking for paper and a pen. 'I don't want us to forget any of the good ideas we come up with on the trip home.'

'Eighteen hours to sit here and think about it?' grinned Dane. 'We're sure to come up with some good stuff.'

'And some crazy stuff,' Lani snorted in amusement. She explained to Amy, 'By the time we've been on here for ten hours, we start getting a bit nutters, and then there are another eight hours to go.'

'I've never been on such a long bus trip,' said Amy, wondering how she'd cope with eighteen hours of travel on a bus.

'You get used to it,' shrugged Lani, 'at least we have plenty of friends on board. Mahalia and Skye are at the back of the bus with their cousins from Charleville, and once the cousins get off at three tomorrow morning, they'll hang with us for the rest of the way. Well, Mahalia will hang with us; Skye will look down her nose at us.'

'Brandon will get on the bus in Toowoomba,' added Dane, missing the expression of interest on his cousin's face. 'He's totally mad to travel with - he'll have us laughing for most of the way home.'

Amy had only met Brandon Suffolk the one time, at the gymkhana on the day Aunt Eleanor and Uncle John presented her with the truck and gooseneck. Lani described him as a rodeo freak, and he did look as though he belonged on the back of a bull, with his western hat, blue jeans, and effortless grace on a horse. Brandon was tall and good-looking, and she remembered his smile that day. He had a beautiful smile and the most amazing dark blue eyes. Not that she liked him or anything, or so she told herself.

'Brandon's a scream,' Lani told her. She'd grown up with him so couldn't see him through Amy's eyes; she just saw the boy she'd always fought with and competed against with their horses. 'He's a total clown. The way he drawls his words would make you wonder if he could even read and write, but he's pretty smart at school. He says he's going to be a vet.'

'Why does he get on in Toowoomba?' asked Amy, hoping to find a balance between sounding too interested in him and appearing as though she didn't like him.

'He goes to school in Warwick,' Dane explained. 'He catches a bus from Warwick up to Toowoomba, which is only about an hour, then he gets this one back to Longreach with the rest of us. We organized it weeks ago. If I have to be on a bus for eighteen hours, I want to have a lunatic like Brandon to keep me entertained.'

'We have to ask him if he'll come hunting the Min Min with us.' Lani spoke the words that Amy secretly willed her to utter. 'I think we should camp out at the gorge for about four days at the least, maybe longer.'

'I'm thinking a whole week,' said Dane, 'we can always drive back to the house if we need anything. If we camp up the northern end, it's only half an hour or so from home.'

Like most outback children, the Winters could drive from the time their feet reached the pedals. They drove the vehicles around the massive property without thinking twice about it. It was what everyone else did, so it was normal to them. Amy still found it strange to think of sitting in a car being driven along the road by ten-year-old Matthew. They pointed out that the roads were only station tracks, so it wasn't much different from someone on a small block of land riding a motorbike around the path they'd built in their paddock.

'If we can convince Brandon to come, that'll be five of us,' said Lani. 'How many tents should we set up?'

Something occurred to Amy, 'I have a better idea. Forget camping out in tents – we have the gooseneck, remember? Lani and I can sleep in the front, and the boys can set up stretchers down the back after the horses are unloaded..'

'Love it!' enthused Lani, thinking of the luxurious living quarters in the front of the gooseneck, including an air conditioner, fridge, television, microwave, and a full-size toilet and shower. 'And we can set the annex up with the table and chairs so we can eat out there. This is going to be the best thing ever!'

It took almost two hours for the bus to reach Toowoomba, and by the time Brandon stepped aboard and sauntered down the center aisle to where Dane had saved him a seat, they had formed most of their plans to find the Min Min lights. Lani waved and grinned at Brandon, then slapped his hand away as he leaned over to tickle her. His dark blue eyes met the green of Amy's, and he winked at her, causing her to blush furiously.

'Hey, bro!' He high-fived Dane and dropped into the

seat beside him. 'Time to get this party on the road. So, how've you all been?'

Before Dane could reply, Lani was leaning over the seat. 'Big news, Brandon – do you want to do the coolest thing ever these holidays?'

Brandon regarded her for a moment before grinning, his eyes twinkling with mischief. 'Do you think you should ask me that while I'm sitting next to your brother, Lani? Sounds like something we should discuss in private.'

Dane burst out laughing, but Lani was less than impressed, 'Oh, yeah, Brandon, like that is ever going to happen. If we were the last people on earth, I'd still find my horse more attractive.'

'Fleet is a good-looking horse,' Brandon conceded, 'but I think I have it over him. What do you think, Amy?'

Amy had joined Lani in leaning over the back of the seats to talk to the boys, but Brandon's question made her want to sink back down and disappear. How could she answer that without appearing awkward? Luckily, no one noticed that she was tongue-tied because Lani rushed on with the news about the search for the Min Min.

'We're going to find the Min Min lights,' she announced before racing on. 'We're taking the horses and Amy's gooseneck, and we'll camp out near the end of Sunhaven Gorge where Uncle John reckons the Min Min hang out. It is going to be totally insane.' She pulled a funny face to emphasize the insanity of the plan. 'Cameras, videos, a full-on investigation, and if we find them, or even if we don't, Amy is going to make a mini-documentary out of it, and we'll make money. You want in?'

'Whoa there,' Brandon raised a hand as though stopping traffic. 'We talk slower down in Warwick than you big city Brisbanites. I think I only understood every third word.'

'You heard me,' Lani narrowed her eyes and pulled a

face at him. 'And just because you talk slower than a gum tree grows doesn't mean you can't understand someone who talks at normal speed.'

'Sixteen hours to go,' interjected Dane, 'let's save some of the fighting for the last few hours, OK?'

Brandon shrugged. Teasing Lani had always been one of his favorite pastimes, but he was happy to save the arguments for the final part of the trip when she would bite even harder when he baited her.

'So, are you in?' Lani repeated.

'Of course, I am. Amy's going to need someone like me to keep her safe from the dragons and black knights.'

That made Lani and Dane chuckle while Amy looked questioningly at them.

'He's going to be your knight in shining armor,' explained Lani. 'Well, technically, he's going to be your Knight on Shining Armour because his full name is Brandon Knight Suffolk and his horse is called Shining Armour. He thinks it makes him pretty crash hot.'

'Yeah, baby.' Brandon winked at Amy again, and they all laughed.

'Of course, the girls have claimed the bedroom up the front,' Dane told him. 'We have to make do with swags down in the horse section.'

'I'm easy,' Brandon shrugged. 'We'll be dry indoors if there's a storm, and I remember seeing a proper bathroom in it as well as a TV, so that beats sleeping in the back of a ute under the stars.'

'So, you don't reckon your parents will stop you from coming?' Dane asked, knowing that Brandon's home life was less than perfect, though he never discussed the problems.

'Nah, they'll be glad to get rid of me after the first few days.' His smile lacked warmth and hinted of troubles at home. 'So, what do you want me to bring, apart from my good looks and humor?'

They began another round of planning, broken by stops at towns along the Warrego Highway as passengers left the bus and, on occasion, joined them. Oakey, Jondaryan, Dalby, and the sun went down. Brigalow, Chinchilla, Goombi, Miles, Drillham, Dulacca, Yuleba, Wallumbilla, Roma, and midnight came and went. The names were familiar to Lani, Dane, and Brandon, but they were uncomfortable on Amy's tongue because she'd grown up with Victorian towns.

After midnight, as the bus hurtled through the darkness, the passengers were quiet, so those who could sleep in the upright seats could have some peace. Lani rested her head on a pillow on her cousin's shoulder, and Amy leaned her forehead against the window and stared out at the moonlit countryside. In six nights' time, according to Brandon's pocket diary, the moon would almost be full. They had decided to start their search for the Min Min on that night, so they could be outside after sunset without needing torches. They intended to do most of their work after dark because no one had ever seen the Min Min in daylight.

Amy went over the pieces of conversation which had danced between the four of them since Brandon joined them at Toowoomba, thinking of all the funny comments she should have made and imagining his response to her amusing remarks. After feeling hopelessly shy for the first hour, unable to participate in the others' nonsense and banter, she began to relax and add her unique style of wit and humor. At times, Brandon looked at her in that approving way, as though they were sharing some secret, which made her feel warm inside.

If she turned her head slightly, she could see the reflection of his face in the window as he watched a movie on his phone, his earphones keeping the sound from disturbing anyone else. The bluish light from the screen lent an eeriness to his profile. His reflection floated on the glass in front of the outback moonscape. Her Knight on Shining Armour, she smiled to herself. Of course, he was only joking, but it sounded good. She began to drift off to sleep, a dark premonition of approaching evil tainting her dreams until an image of Brandon rode in to protect her.

*****

Jake, Skinner, and Meat

On a poorly lit road near Brisbane, a lean, hungry-looking woman stood by a white four-wheel-drive wagon. Staring down the road, she rolled the keys around one of her tattooed fingers as she chewed gum and waited. Lights approached. She stepped back into her vehicle and locked the doors, bending over so a passing motorist wouldn't see her.

The car stopped behind her, the motor still running, and a gruff voice called, 'Jess – it's us.'

She sat up and quickly started the engine, unlocked the doors, and climbed out to see three men approaching at a run.

'Everything's packed,' she told them as they flung open the doors and scrambled in. 'There's money an' stuff in the glove box. You keep going.'

'Dump the car down New South Wales somewhere,' the driver told her as he settled into the seat, slamming the door shut before winding the window down. 'Only fuel up at little places, and don't stop anywhere else. Hide your face from any cameras. Clean the prints out before you dump it. Got that?'

She handed him a mobile phone, 'Got it. You all be careful.'

'We'll do what it takes,' the driver told her coldly. 'I'll call you when we've found a place. Better you don't know where we're going.'

The white four-wheel-drive accelerated away. The woman, following instructions, took the car and headed towards New South Wales. She drove to Boonah, crossed the border on the Lions Road, and found a remote place many hundreds of kilometers away where she could leave the car for the police to find. After that, she caught a bus back to Brisbane. She did some shopping in town before going home as though it was a typical day, and when the police came knocking, she acted surprised, swore at them as she usually did, and convinced them she knew nothing.

A massive search would be launched because three escaped murderers were headline news, but she knew her brother would manage to stay one jump ahead of the police.

HORSES OF THE LIGHT

CHAPTER TWO
Home Again

'See you in a few days,' Dane told Brandon as he, Lani, and Amy made their way out of the bus at Longreach, eighteen hours after boarding in Brisbane.

'Don't forget to bring those movies, or you're dead.' Lani waved a finger threateningly at him.

'I'll miss you too, Lani.' He grinned at her. 'See you, Amy.'

'Bye, Brandon,' she nodded as she followed Lani down the aisle to the front door of the bus.

'Christmas Eve at our place,' Mahalia Wren reminded them. After her cousins left the bus at Charleville, she sat with them, and they made plans for things to do after the Min Min hunt was over. The Christmas Eve party at Wren's property was a long-standing tradition in the area. The Winters hadn't missed since they were born.

'Wish you'd come looking for the Min Min with us,' Lani called to her as she was about to step off the bus.

'If I can make it, I'll let you know. I'll come over with

Brandon if I can, but I think we have visitors, so I probably won't get there.' She waved out the window as she saw Mrs. Winter approach to welcome her children home.

Eleanor Winter smiled up at Brandon and Mahalia and placed a hand over her heart before pointing to them. She'd known them since they were babies and loved them with that same warm, all-encompassing love that she gave to all around her.

The dry heat of the Longreach air sucked the moisture from Amy's lungs as she stepped out of the air-conditioned bus. It was to be her first summer in the outback and, though everyone warned her about the heat, it still shocked her when she felt the full force of hot air hit her like the blast from a furnace. She realized that her plans for working horses all summer had been somewhat rash when swimming in the creek was much more sensible in this weather.

Eleanor swept the three arrivals up into her arms for a hug. 'We're all together again!' she announced joyfully. 'It's so good to have you home.'

'Where's Matthew?' Lani asked, wondering why he wasn't there to greet them. Since their father died a few months ago, she found herself wanting to keep tabs on her family members.

'He's just being Matthew.' Her mother shook her head, smiling. 'He went to buy a drink then thought of something else and promised he'd be here when the bus pulled in. He's probably yakking to someone about horses and has forgotten.'

'I haven't forgotten!' cried Matthew as he ran to them, catching his mother's last words. He threw himself at his brother, sister, and cousin with his usual level of enthusiasm, knocking them several steps back along the pavement. 'Boring days are over – the gang's all here!'

'So, what's news?' Dane draped an arm around his brother's shoulders and gave him a gentle shake.

'You get all the news every day,' said Matthew, referring to the fact that they stayed in contact daily on social media and their phones.

'Yeah, but you don't tell me everything. What haven't you told me?'

Matthew narrowed his eyes, thinking hard for something to tell his brother that he hadn't already shared in a phone conversation, Facebook, Instagram, Twitter, an email, or text. 'There's a top-knot pigeon nesting outside my window, and her two babies look like aliens.'

'Big googly eyes?' asked Dane, laughing as he remembered the look of baby pigeons.

'Like huge bulging balls with a little body attached,' agreed Matthew. 'Look, I have a photo.'

As Matthew searched his phone for the images of the googly-eyed pigeons, Dane collected the suitcases and told his mother about their trip.

'No problems, just seventeen hours too long, as usual,' he complained, 'but Brandon kept us laughing.'

'Mahalia sat with us after her cousins got off at Charleville,' said Lani. 'She said she might get over next week for the camping trip we've planned.'

'Camping, are we?' Mrs. Winter quizzed them. 'How do you feel about camping, Amy?'

'Lani and I are going to have the beds in the gooseneck,' Amy smirked at Matthew, who had stopped, phone in hand, to stare at them eagerly. 'Dane, Brandon, and Matthew can camp down the back in the horse section.'

Matthew punched the air with a fist, 'Yeah! Camping.'

'If it's OK with you, of course, Mum,' Dane gave his mother a winning look, knowing full well that he could charm her into agreeing with their plans.

'So, it's not so much roughing it in tents out in the wilds as enjoying all the comforts of home.' She gave her son an amused smile.

'Beats swags on green ant nests,' Dane grinned at her, 'like in your good old days.'

'We were tough in our day,' Mrs. Winter agreed with a lop-sided smile. 'We slept on beds of cactus with lumps of wood for pillows. You youngsters are just spoiled.'

'So, where are we camping?' asked Matthew as he shoved his phone under Dane's nose and rushed on. 'Here are the pigeons.'

'Cool, bro,' Dane looked at the photo and then proceeded to flick through the other images, passing remarks on each one, to the delight of Matthew, who worshipped his brother, particularly after a long absence at school.

'Where are you going to camp?' Mrs. Winter asked Lani and Amy as they carried suitcases back to the car. 'Though I use the word lightly…it doesn't seem that sleeping in the gooseneck is really like camping.'

'Just out near the end of Sunhaven Gorge,' Lani told her. 'There are some great places to walk, and we have radio contact with the house from there.'

They decided not to tell Mrs. Winter that they intended to look for the Min Min lights. Like many who lived in Min Min territory, she knew of them and had a deep respect for them but preferred to leave them alone and pretend they didn't exist. Adults didn't need to know they were looking for the Min Min, Lani told herself. After all, they could just as easily be camping in the same place without wanting to find the mysterious lights, and it was unlikely they would find them anyway.

'And I want to see what Legend's Leap looks like when I'm at the bottom looking fifty meters up,' said Amy, 'rather than jumping over it looking down, wondering if I'll fall fifty meters.'

'I still can't believe you did that,' Lani shook her head. 'No one even knows if our great-grandad really did the leap on his horse or if that's just a story, but we all know you and Laddie jumped it. I can't even stand near the edge.'

They were all aware that they were talking about the night Geoff Winter died, but Mrs. Winter urged them to talk about it for all the right reasons, and the incredible ride by Amy was an excellent reason to remember it.

'Will you take your horses?' Eleanor asked as they reached the car and began loading up the luggage.

'Absolutely,' Lani nodded. 'We've got the portable yards, and Dane and Brandon said they'd run some wires between the trees to make some bigger runs for them.'

'I'll take Blaze as well,' said Amy, thinking of the young kelpie at home on Sunhaven Downs. It had been one of her chores to feed the sheepdogs, and she'd become attached to the young yellow-eyed, red dog, teaching him tricks and letting him accompany her everywhere. Her mother had never allowed her to have a dog, so she was overjoyed when Aunt Eleanor said that Blaze had decided he was her dog, so she'd better have him. 'I bought a book about training dogs, and he's going to be the best-trained dog ever.'

'Gooseneck, horses, dog, friends... it sounds like you have it all planned out. Am I allowed to join you?'

'That would be great, Mum,' Dane said with false enthusiasm, his mind ticking over for a way to deter his mother. 'If you're there, you can do all the cooking and washing for us. Thanks for that.'

'Good one,' chuckled Matthew.

'Nice move.' Mrs. Winter nodded her appreciation of his attempt to manipulate her and threatened back with, 'I might just take you up on your offer.'

After their things were in the car, they drove down Eagle Street to the supermarket to buy cold goods before heading home. Eleanor and Matthew had brought the portable freezer to town to stock up on frozen foods and ice cream. With a trip of several hours ahead of them to the station, they needed a freezer that ran off the car's battery to ensure the food remained frozen. They already had several boxes of groceries in the back of the vehicle and had left the cold goods until it was time to leave town.

They talked so much on the trip home that the two hours passed quickly. As they crossed the Thomson River outside Longreach, Matthew excitedly pointed out how much water was in the weir, which led to a discussion about how good the season had been since the drought broke with the unseasonal storms back in September. Mrs. Winter insisted it was merely a reprieve from the drought, and the lack of rain since did not bode well for the season.

As they passed various stations, the Winters regaled Amy with information about the people who lived there. It seemed that in an area almost the size of the state of Victoria, everyone knew everyone else. They even knew the sports they played, their schools, who they were related to, and the names of their horses.

'They have three boys, all at Nudgee,' Dane told her as they passed one station, 'and they have a good Quarter Horse stallion who's thrown some top polocrosse horses, but they're more into reining than anything else.'

'The Schmidts only bought this place three years ago,' Eleanor explained about another property, marked by a mailbox the size of a small car next to a dirt track that ran off the bitumen. 'They come from down the river near Tocal, and they still have a property down there. They breed Santa Gertrudis, those big red cattle, and are somehow related to Brandon's family - the people, that is, not the cattle. I think their grandparents were cousins or something like that. One of their jackaroos won lotto last year, almost two million dollars, and bought a station of his own.'

'He thought he'd make a small fortune on the land,' quipped Dane, 'by starting with a large fortune.'

Every property passed came with a snippet of information about the people, their animals, and the property itself. Amy was quite entertained by how much they knew about everyone else.

They turned south off the Landsborough Highway onto a dirt road before Winton and traveled the unfenced track through half a dozen properties. They slowed for the cattle grids placed in the road where fences crossed it. Cars could drive over them, but the stock could not walk across the metal bars set more than a hoof distance apart. Each paddock they went through ranged from a couple of kilometers to ten kilometers across, and the Mitchell and Flinders grasses were lush and green, a massive change from the parched land that Amy first saw some months earlier.

After turning onto a less used track, they could see the Sunhaven Hills in the distance. Lani's and Dane's eyes glowed as they stared at the thirty-kilometer-long, narrow line of flat-topped hills that marked the boundary between their property and Uncle John's station, Brindella Fells. They passed over a grid, and the Winters all cried, 'Home!' because they had just driven on to Sunhaven land.

Soon they reached the Sunhaven mailbox, a set of forty-four-gallon drums set up like two galloping horses, and they turned into the driveway. The homestead was about five kilometers from the road, so it wasn't like any driveway Amy had known when she lived in Melbourne.

Amy sensed the growing excitement in Dane and Lani, and she shared in that wonderful feeling of coming home after a term at boarding school, something that all children who live on outback stations know. It was like being a wild bird locked in a small cage for too long. Now the door was opening, and they were about to fly free again.

When the car approached the homestead, marked by the big trees in the garden in a landscape of smaller, hardy native trees, no one mentioned that they were crossing the spot where Geoff Winter had died in the car roll-over some months earlier, but they were all thinking it. Lani looked out the window, and Amy noticed her hand going up to her face to wipe away the tears.

'Home again,' Mrs. Winter broke the silence brought on by memories of Geoff as she stopped the car at the garden gate of the homestead. 'What are you going to do first? See the horses?'

'Bathroom first,' yelled Lani, racing towards the house, 'and then the horses.'

'Horses first,' said Dane as he headed towards the stables. 'There's a handy tree down here for me.'

'So gross,' Amy wrinkled her nose up at him. She had grown up an only child and wasn't used to the ways of boys. Before she could say anything else, a leaping, yipping red bullet of a dog hit her legs. Blaze almost knocked her over with the excitement of seeing her again.

'Hey, a bean's a bean, but a pee's a relief,' Dane grinned at her, walking backward, his hands out by his side in a *what can you do?* pose.

She pulled a face at him and followed Lani into the house. Blaze trotted at her heels, gazing up at her adoringly, his intelligent kelpie face split by a happy smile.

Despite the heat, the girls changed into riding clothes and headed to the stables while Mrs. Winter set about making a late lunch for them. The stables, horse yards, and riding arena lay across the big quadrangle from the house. The workers' cottages and the big machinery shed closed the other two sides of the square. The grassed square was an excellent place for playing ball games or showing off horses if buyers came looking.

They found Dane leading his mare, Misty, out of the stables while Matthew sat sideways on his horse, Shandy, in the breezeway, chattering away to his brother. The stables were fifteen degrees cooler than the outside temperature because of the shade trees and a simple but ingenious watering system. Sprinklers sprayed water on the iron roof before it ran down canvas panels outside to gather in a cement pond. It was like a giant Coolgardie safe – an old cooling device for food that relied on the cooling properties of evaporating water. On the hottest of days, the stables were comfortable for the horses.

'I put them all in the stables early this morning before we went to town,' he told the girls, 'and I've lunged them every day for the last ten days, so they're fit and ready to ride. I lunged them all yesterday with their saddles on, and no one's lame or sore – Laddie did buck a bit with the saddle on, but he was only playing.'

'You're a champion, bro,' Dane grinned at him and gave his leg a gentle slap as he led Misty past. He fastened his helmet, put the reins over Misty's head, and vaulted easily onto her back. 'I win,' he called to the girls, 'I'm the first one on my horse after getting home.'

'Pig's bum, you win,' Lani told him. 'There was no competition to win. If there was, I won at being first in the house, and Amy won at being first to pull on riding boots.'

'Seems like we're all winners, then,' he called as he trotted Misty out onto the sandy surface of the riding arena. 'Hurry up and get out here with your horses.'

Like Dane and Matthew, the girls put snaffle bridles on their horses and rode out bareback, Lani on her grey gelding, Fleet, and Amy on her big palomino gelding, Days. Fleet played polocrosse, went to pony club, and mustered and, at 14.3 hands, was a handy size for Lani, who adored him. Images of him covered her school books, and she had entire photo albums filled with shots of Fleet. Amy had three horses: Jack and Days were seasoned eventing horses, while Laddie was the Sunhaven bred Thoroughbred that she hoped would be her Olympic eventer in years to come.

After mounting and walking their horses around for a minute, the girls cantered after Dane and Matthew. The boys had ridden out into the paddock towards the back fence of the House Paddock, over a kilometer away.

'We should do this every time we come home from school,' Dane announced as they halted their horses on a small rise and looked back at the homestead buildings. The line of Sunhaven Hills stood tall behind them, their flat tops shimmering in the heat haze. Despite the extreme heat of the early afternoon, the horses didn't appear to be sweating because the dry air sucked any moisture off them the instant it appeared.

'Good idea,' agreed Lani, patting Fleet's neck. 'Being on Fleet out here makes those months of boarding school seem a whole universe away.'

'I still can't believe that I'm on Days in the middle of the outback,' said Amy, lying along the neck of white mane. 'Four months ago, I barely knew you guys existed, then life went crazy for a while, and now everything's back in place, but I'm in a whole new world.'

'I still can't believe your Mum sold your horses,' Lani shook her head, her green eyes meeting the matching green eyes of her cousin. 'It must have killed you that day you saw them driven away in someone else's float.'

'It felt like someone stole all my dreams.' Amy buried her face into Days' mane and breathed in the essence of horse which gave her so much strength. 'Days and Jack weren't just horses - they were everything good about life.'

They also helped connect Amy to her father, who had died years earlier in South America. Knowing that Amy's mother had little interest in helping her daughter achieve her ambition of competing internationally, he had made sure there was money set aside for her to have her horses and lessons and go on competing. Amy often joked that if it'd been up to her mother and Nikos, her stepfather, the only horse she would have had anything to do with was a pottery horse made a thousand years ago, which they'd found on a dig in China.

'Now you've got all of us,' chirped Matthew happily, 'and all of this,' his arm swept around the vast landscape of Sunhaven Downs, 'which means, of course, that when your Mum comes back in a year, you're going to have to ask her if you can stay on with us.'

'We're not going to let you go,' Lani told her. 'Look at you, sitting bareback on your eventing horse in the middle of the outback – you belong here.'

'I feel like I belong,' Amy smiled at her cousins, 'I hadn't even thought about staying on, but it's a pretty good idea.'

'It's a great idea,' enthused Lani. 'You go to one of the best boarding schools in the country. You can have all the holidays out here with the horses and us. Your Mum and Nikos don't have to worry about you while they're digging up ruins overseas - you can have a week or two with them each year when it's convenient for them.'

Amy laughed, 'Sounds like you have it all worked out.'

'I've been thinking of it for weeks,' Lani confessed, then rushed on with the next part of her plan. 'I'm going to ask

Mum if we can take our horses to school with us. Maybe not this year, but in a year or so when we're older and need to be riding them every week and not just during the holidays. I spoke to Mrs. Belby about it, and she said we'd get on the school equestrian team, and we'd probably even get a sporting scholarship to help cover the costs, which would make our parents happy.'

Mrs. Belby, one of the teachers at school, ran the equestrian program, which allowed students to keep their horses at a nearby training center, train on weekends and after school, and compete in various horse sports.

'I want to take Shandy with me when I go to school,' said Matthew, patting his horse's chestnut neck. 'Why haven't I heard this before? Why don't you have Misty and Fleet there?'

'It costs a heap to have horses down in Brisbane, bro,' Dane told him, 'and I guess I never really thought about it before. You'd want to be serious about competing, like Amy, before thinking about it.'

'You guys ride as well as me, if not better,' Amy pointed out. 'If you decide to get serious about competing in something, you're going to get to the top if you work at it. Want to come eventing with me?'

Dane shook his head, 'Nah, the dressage part doesn't exactly thrill me. I'm too hooked on polocrosse – flat gallop down the field cradling the ball is a bit more exciting than tracking left at C and trotting ten-meter circles at E.'

'Well, see if you can do polocrosse at school, then,' said Amy, thinking of all the horse sports that would suit Dane, 'or campdrafting or cutting or reining or something exciting like that, but, I'm telling you, for excitement, nothing beats the rush of a cross country course.'

'Cross country is great,' agreed Dane, 'no arguments there, I'm just not into dressage.'

'Reining,' nodded Matthew, a faraway look in his eyes, remembering something he'd forgotten until that point. 'You know, I had a dream the other night that I was reining on a palomino.'

'On Days?' Amy smiled and patted the palomino neck. 'He's never had a go at it, but he might like those big sliding stops, you never know.'

'Nah,' Matthew laughed, looking at the sixteen-hand horse that made Amy look tiny up on top of him, 'anyone can see he's built to jump and gallop over cross country. Mine was a smaller horse with a mane down past his neck. It seemed real, like I really was on a horse spinning and sliding and reining back. I know I loved the horse, and everyone was cheering and stomping...' His voice faded away as he relived the dream. 'It seemed so real.'

'Maybe it's going to be real,' Amy said gently. 'Perhaps he's in your future, waiting for you.'

'Hope so,' Matthew murmured, still moved by the strength of feeling stirred by memories of the dream of his horse, the reining palomino.

'I'll tell you about the future,' said Dane, as he picked up his reins and began to walk back towards the homestead. 'Mum is in the house wondering where we are and thinking we'd better be in soon for the late lunch she was making for us, and if we don't get back, our future is going to be bleak... no Min Min hunting if we upset Mum.'

He closed his legs on Misty's side, and she made a seamless transition from a walking stride to a canter stride, and he moved with her as though they were one, his reins light in one hand, his other hand hanging loosely at his side.

Matthew jammed his heels into Shandy's side, and he jumped forward from a halt to a fast canter to catch up with Dane as he called, 'What do you mean about a Min Min hunt? I want to hunt the Min Min.'

Both the girls urged their horses forward and joined the boys, the four horses cantering effortlessly over the Mitchell grass tussocks as Dane explained to his brother about the motive behind the camping trip they had planned.

'But don't tell Mum,' Lani told him as they slipped off their horses at the stables and put them in the loose boxes with some hay to eat. 'It's not a big deal or anything, but Mum's pretty cluey, she'll realize that the Min Min only come out at night, so if we're looking for them, it means we'll be out wandering around at night, and she's not going to like that.'

'There's going to be a full moon,' added Dane, 'so it will be nearly as light as during the day, anyway. It's not like it's going to be dangerous or anything.'

'We've ridden our horses by the light of the moon plenty of times,' said Lani, 'but you know how Mum will worry if she thinks of us riding around at night when we're ten kilometers away.'

'I get it,' Matthew raised his hand to stop their explanations and justifications. 'You could have stopped at, Don't tell Mum. I'm not going to blab to her, and I know we'll be safe.'

As soon as the horses were settled in their stables with the water checked and hay shared, they went back to the house to enjoy the air-conditioned comfort of a late lunch in the kitchen, planning the things they'd do for the next few days before they went looking for the Min Min. Mrs. Winter had chores for them all, there was a day planned for Christmas shopping in town, and they wanted to work the horses in the early mornings and late afternoons. Life was busy at the station.

It was the perfect start to Amy's best Christmas holidays ever, but as the days sped by, she felt uneasy, as though something was approaching from behind, but when she looked, she couldn't see it. Each morning, a murder of crows set up a loud chorus near the house, and she shivered when she heard them. Crows meant death, she knew that, and she wondered for whom they called.

*****

Violence at Lake Bindegolly

The three men in the four-wheel-drive followed back roads as they meandered through Queensland, heading west from Brisbane. The main driver, Jake, studied maps and marked out routes that would keep them away from towns wherever possible, and they listened to the news as reports of their suspected whereabouts were issued. The car they'd stolen when they first broke out of prison was found burnt out in the Dorrigo National Park in New South Wales, prompting theories that they were headed to Victoria where the two cousins, Meat and Skinner, had family members.

They used the camping equipment provided by Jess to stay at isolated spots by rivers or dams where three fishermen would not look out of place. They had a night at Nindigully and camped near the Warrego River out near Cunamulla, where they caught Yellowbelly fish and joked about the police looking for them in Victoria. The following day, they headed further west towards Lake Bindegolly, where they intended to spend a week or more before heading to the Territory and, finally, over to Western Australia.

'It's gunna be a new life for us,' said Skinner, as he bobbed his fishing line in the lake.

'I ain't never goin' back to prison, that's for sure,' nodded Meat, whose massive, fleshy hands had helped give rise to his nickname. 'I'm tellin' ya - I'm gunna die before I go back there.'

'Or someone else will,' quipped Skinner, sending them into peals of laughter.

'Keep it down, will ya!' Jake ordered, 'There's a car comin' down the track. No more prison talk – we're just three blokes having a holiday in the outback, right?'

'Sure, Jake,' Meat and Skinner agreed, nodding emphatically.

They were sitting with fishing rods in hand when a Landcruiser pulled up, and a middle-aged man emerged, a friendly smile on his face.

'Hey there – a good day for some fishing!' he called as he approached. 'What's the fishing like here?'

Jake put on a forced smile and replied, 'Nuthin' much bitin' yet, but we're hoping to land a few. There was good fishing back at Nindigully, though, if you's after some fish.'

'I've already been through there early this morning. I'm heading home to Nockatunga after almost a month down in the big smoke. Thought I might just throw a line in as a bit of a welcome home to my part of the world. Where do you boys hail from?'

'Here and there,' said Jake, wishing the man would go on his way.

'Yo!' the visitor exclaimed with a broad smile as he looked at Skinner's fishing line suddenly bend over. 'Looks like you've got one. A big one.'

Skinner snarled something at him and began to land the fish, playing him gently so that he didn't break the line. When at last he pulled out a three-kilo Yellowbelly, he held it up like a trophy and showed the others.

'Good catch,' commented the visitor, who then stepped forward to offer his hand in a friendly manner. He'd been born and bred in the outback and liked making visitors feel welcome in his little corner of the world. 'My name's Bob.

Bob McMahon.'

Jake shook his hand firmly, noticing how Bob's eyes lingered on the prison tattoos on his arm, and offered up the names of John, Matt, and Ryan. He wanted Bob to leave but not take any suspicions with him. He knew that in this sort of country, everyone knew everyone else, and it might only take a quick word to the local police officer about the three unfriendly men out by the lake to make the police come and pay a visit to check on them.

Bob's attention moved to another line that jiggled as a fish nibbled at the bait, 'Looks like you've picked a darned good spot,' he told them and stepped closer to the edge of the water to watch the line, his hands itching to take the rod and land the fish himself. Perhaps these fellows wouldn't mind him sharing their spot for a while, he thought; he sure would enjoy dropping a line in after being away so long. He didn't notice that Meat had picked up a piece of wood from next to their car, a hardwood pick handle that Jess had packed as a weapon.

'So, you boys headed further west?' Bob asked, his eyes on the fishing rod that was bending as the fish took the bait.

He didn't have any warning before the wood hit the side of his head with a sickening sound. His body crumpled to the ground.

'He was asking too many questions,' muttered Meat, looking down at Bob with cold eyes. He was no stranger to killing, and he felt nothing, no emotion at all, no more than if he'd swatted a fly.

'Yeah, well, he's not goin' to be asking any now,' sniffed Jake, pushing at Bob's body with his boot. 'Better get a move on, now.'

'What do we do with him?' asked Skinner, reeling in the second fish as though nothing unusual had happened.

'Just leave him,' said Jake. 'No one's likely to find him in the next day or two. Get our stuff in the car, and we'll get goin' so we can get some miles between us and this place.'

They threw their gear into their vehicle, packing the two fish into an icebox. After putting on a pair of gloves, Jake went through Bob's car, removing his wallet and suitcase and anything else he thought could be of use to them. He used his tools to pull off some spare parts from the engine which might be handy, including the battery, which he placed in the back of their car.

'Should we head back to Brisbane?' Meat asked as he climbed into the passenger seat next to Jake.

'Our best chance is still out here, I reckon, not the city.' Jake nodded at the vast expanse of the outback as he started the engine and gave one last look at Bob's body in the dust before hitting the accelerator. 'We'll head north a bit before crossing into the Territory.'

He spun the wheels and sped away, sending out a plume of dust that shrouded Bob. No one noticed that Bob's eyes opened as they left. *Heading north,* he thought through the aching pain in his head, *they're heading north, then to the Territory.* He didn't know who they were, but he knew he had to inform the police. If only he could get help. He closed his eyes again.

CHAPTER THREE
Going Camping

The Meeting Room, a small shed at the back of the Sunhaven gardens, provided privacy for the three Winters and Amy to discuss their search for the Min Min lights. It was hidden in the rain forest section of the gardens and was a 'no adults' zone, something Mrs. Winter respected, avoiding the area whenever a meeting took place. When they had been younger, they called it the Cubby House, but they were far too sophisticated now to hang out in a cubby, so it was re-named the Meeting Room.

Inside, there was a large wooden table with a collection of chairs around it. Blue carpet covered most of the cement floor, and there were a couple of pet rugs thrown down for Blaze, who lay watching Amy, his tongue lolling as he panted in the early morning heat. There was a bench along one wall for food and drinks, which they brought down from the house, and images of horses cut from magazines covered the walls.

They wanted to go over last-minute plans before Brandon arrived at lunchtime. They planned to spend four nights away, and that took some serious organizing.

'First up - Mum has worked out all the food,' Lani said. She moved a sheet of paper from in front of her to the center of the table. 'Here's her list, if you want to have a look. She reckons it's enough to feed an army, so we won't need to come home for extra supplies.'

Matthew pulled the list over and gave it a quick scan, 'Yep, plenty of healthy food there that Mum knows we won't eat.' He snorted in amusement at some of the items, 'Yeah, good one, Mum – like we're going to eat the frozen vegetable casserole when we have chips, sausages, and hot dogs.'

'I like your Mum's vege casserole,' Amy defended the dish.

'Cool – it's all yours,' Matthew gave her his cheeky grin. 'Problem sol-ved.' He broke the word into two syllables. He liked to deliberately mispronounce words and then wait to see if people corrected him. The other three knew better than to correct him.

'Mum will come out and visit us tomorrow to make sure we survive tonight,' continued Lani, 'and I guess she'll check to see what we've been eating.'

'I can save her the trouble and tell her now,' Matthew nodded at the others. 'We'll eat the junk food, Amy will have the vege stuff, Blaze will eat some of the healthy things, and the Min Min lights can have the rest. I vote we make food sacrifices of all the healthy food.'

He raised his hand and waited for his brother to reward his plan with a high five.

'Food all settled,' Dane slapped Matthew's hand and met him grin for grin. 'Also, step one for contacting the Min Min – leave the wholesome food out for them while we suffer eating the Winter basic food groups diet.'

Amy raised her brows at her cousins, wondering what

constituted that diet.

'The three basic food groups,' Lani laughed as she explained, holding up three fingers. 'Salt, fat, sugar. It's something we came up with last Christmas holidays when Mum went on the rampage about healthy eating and the five basic food groups – the proper ones, that is. She even put up a poster in the kitchen about it, so Matthew, twit that he is, made up a poster to put over the top of it called the Three Basic Winter Food Groups. He cut out photos of junk food and divided them up into salt, fat, and sugar.'

'With a lot of overlapping,' pointed out Matthew proudly. 'It was very complicated. I think it was a work of genius for a nine-year-old.'

He put up his hand for another high five from his brother, but Dane only shook his head and held his hand to the side. 'Sorry, bro, can't reward acts of vanity. It was funny, but not genius. Now, the UFO kites, they were genius.' He slapped Matthew's hand on that.

'Oh, that was so funny,' chortled Lani, remembering the incident. 'So, so, so funny. And, yes, I think it was brilliant, too. Probably your best ever, Matty – I think your brains peaked for that, and it's going to be all downhill from there.'

'UFO kites?' Amy looked from one to the other, puzzled.

'You'll love this,' Lani began. 'It was about eighteen months ago in the mid-year holidays, and some woman who went to school with Mum, Maree, came out with her husband and their kids.'

'And that is an insult to baby goats,' cut in Matthew.

'They were one hundred and ten percent feral little rats,' agreed Lani. 'Jason, the husband, kept telling us how wonderful his children were, and how smart they were, and how talented.'

'It was sickening,' said Matthew, putting his fingers in his mouth and making gagging noises.

'Jason and Maree looked down their noses at everything we had,' Lani shook her head. 'Their cars were better, their house was better, they had better computers, and better sprinkles for their doughnuts. Everything they had was better than ours.'

Dane chuckled at Lani's words and took up the story, 'One night, we were all talking about the Min Min lights. Jason said they were nonsense - stories made up by country yokels to entertain children. He didn't believe in anything like that: no UFOs, no Min Mins, no ghosts, or heaven, or anything apart from what you could see with your eyes and buy with money.'

'So, Dr. Evil Genius,' Lani indicated Matthew, 'had the best idea ever. We had these little strips of colored LED lights that flashed in patterns, and he glued them to a couple of kites. We knew that Jason had to have a smoke outside before going to bed, so one night after everyone else had gone to bed, we snuck outside with the kites and launched them. There wasn't much wind, but it was enough to get the kites going well. We were out in the paddock, making them duck and dive and hover.'

'We could see Jason's cigarette on the veranda,' Dane took over once more, 'going up and down as he smoked, then it froze. He must have just stood there like a statue staring at our UFOs for a minute, and then he yelped because the cigarette burned his fingers.'

'We were trying not to laugh,' chortled Matthew at the memory. 'We had those kites dancing in the sky. All he would have seen were these flashing lights skimming around like space ships. He ran inside and yelled for everyone to come out, so we brought the kites down and bolted back to bed. No one else saw them, and there he was trying to tell them that he did see them.'

'Yeah, it was a classic,' said Dane. 'There was Mr. I-don't-believe-in-any-of-that-nonsense going on and on about the UFOs he'd seen that night.'

'It would have been better,' proposed Matthew, his eyes narrowed with thought, 'if we had a loudspeaker so we could have given him a message from the aliens.'

'Something like, Give all your money to Matthew?' Amy asked him.

'Something like that,' he grinned back at her.

'We have to take the UFO kites out with us,' said Lani. 'Brandon hasn't seen them yet, and he'll love them.'

'Added to the list,' Dane wrote UFO kites on a piece of paper in front of him. 'OK. Back to business. Horse feed – Matthew?'

'All packed up in the back of the truck,' Matthew held up his list so everyone could see he had worked it out properly. 'Five horses, half a bale a day each, four days, that's ten bales, and I added a couple of spares. Plus, two bags of workhorse mix. Feed bins, water buckets, and I filled up the water storage with tank water for us because we'll be parked next to the bore so that the horses will have water there.'

They continued working through their lists. It was the first time they'd spent more than a single night camping by themselves. They were determined to prove to Mrs. Winter that they could manage by themselves, and being well-organized was part of the proof.

It wasn't as though there was any danger, thought Amy, as she wondered about the four days ahead. They weren't leaving Sunhaven, and they were only a radio call away from home. They could drive back to the house in less than half an hour. It was as safe as kids in the city, setting up a tent in their back yard. Or so she told herself, but she couldn't shake the sense of foreboding that hung at the back of her mind like a black mist on the horizon.

They wandered back to the house, satisfied they had everything packed and prepared, and waited for Brandon to arrive. Their horses were in the stables, ready to load on the gooseneck parked in the quadrangle. They had completed their chores for the day, so they weren't leaving much work for Mrs. Winter while they were away. They were ready to go.

Dane had one more check of the weather on the internet to ensure they had fine days ahead. They hadn't faced storms since the unseasonal monster which killed their father in their last holidays, and he did not want to be away from the house, or their mother, if storms hit. The prediction was for hot and dry days.

'Dust coming!' Lani called from the veranda.

'Were Brandon's parents bringing him over?' Mrs. Winter asked the children.

'I think he's driving himself,' answered Dane, a little uncomfortably. They all knew that Brandon's home life was less than happy, but they didn't know how to help apart from having Brandon over whenever possible. His father didn't socialize much, and there were no invitations to visit Brandon's house, so they thought it wasn't a happy household. He often joked about not getting along with his parents, but they all suspected that it was something that hurt him deeply.

Mrs. Winter nodded. She understood that there were problems in the Suffolk family, and she always welcomed Brandon in their home. All children need at least one place where they feel loved and wanted, even if that wasn't their own home, and Mrs. Winter made sure Brandon knew he had that at Sunhaven. She believed that he'd grow up fine. He was smart and had a good sense of humor, and, most importantly, he appeared to be strong in spirit. He wouldn't let problems at home crush the dreams out of him. It was a blessing that Brandon's grandparents paid for him to be at boarding school in Warwick for most of the year so that he didn't have too much time at home.

Within a few minutes, an old battered ute pulling an equally dilapidated horse float pulled up near the gooseneck. Brandon climbed out and waved to everyone. 'I'd have come earlier if I'd known you were going to be standing around waiting for me,' he drawled, then granted Mrs. Winter one of his disarming smiles. 'Morning, Mrs. Winter, you're looking beautiful, as usual.'

She laughed like a young girl at his compliment. He could charm the sparrows from the trees, she thought, and in a few years, she might be a little concerned about her girls heading out on a camping trip with him. For now, though, she knew they were safe. His pleasant manners and teasing ways had not yet given way to the rising tide of hormones that made the older teenage boys look at girls in a different light from the friendly, bantering way he saw Lani and Amy. Although, Eleanor paused in her thoughts and looked closely at the pink stain on her niece's cheeks, it appeared that Amy might be seeing Brandon in a less than a brotherly light.

'Thank you, Brandon,' she smiled warmly at him and held her arms out to hug him. 'How was the drive over?'

'I drove her like she was stolen, Mrs. Double-you,' he quipped. He often shortened her name to his pet version of the pronunciation of the letter 'W.' On one of his stays at Sunhaven, many years earlier, when he was only seven or eight, he had written a small poem for Mrs. Winter. It finished with the lines, 'The only way the world could be better, Mrs. W., was if we had double you.' Since then, he had written his Christmas and birthday cards to her as Mrs.

Double-you, and Eleanor hoped he would never grow out of calling her that.

'That's never likely to happen,' snorted Dane, looking at the ramshackle old ute. 'No one is going to try and steal that.'

'Old Gertrude has a million clicks left in her,' Brandon defended the old ute his father let him drive around the station. 'She'd be a prize for any thief, well, if he could ever get her started, that is. She's a bit touchy about turning over these days. She has one good start a day in her, and then she can refuse to start until the next day.'

As they talked, Amy marveled about the fact that someone who was only fourteen could drive almost fifty kilometers in a ute by himself, pulling a horse float. Seeing teens her age and just a year older driving cars still amused her. She knew they all grew up in the outback driving vehicles as soon as they could reach the pedals and that they were careful not to break any laws by only driving on private property. Out here, on the enormous stations, that meant they could travel hundreds of kilometers without ever having to cross onto a government road, but it still seemed strange.

Her cousins showed her how to drive one of the station vehicles, but she was still shaky on the gear changes and using the clutch properly. It disheartened her as they all seemed to drive as well as most adults she had known. Better, perhaps. Even ten-year-old Matthew had no problem driving around the station, checking the stock waters, and he needed to sit on a cushion so that he could see over the steering wheel.

'Which horse did you bring?' Lani asked him. 'That doesn't look like Shine's head in the window, so I guess you aren't going to be our Knight on Shining Armour.'

'I'll always be that,' he grinned at Lani and Amy. 'But,

you're right. Shine's at home, and I've brought Nu-man.' Brandon stepped to the back of the float to pat the well-muscled chestnut hindquarter of the Shiny And Nu gelding his grandfather had given him as a weanling two years earlier. 'I started him in the last holidays myself and brought him back in a few days ago. He's so smart that I reckon he'll be reading and writing by the New Year.'

'You going to rodeo him?' Dane asked, peering into the float at the solid Quarter Horse with kind eyes and an intelligent head. Brandon had been going to rodeos with his father from the day he could hang on to the rope of a poddy calf and ride it for more than a few seconds. Mr. Suffolk had some handy team ropers. He was also a pick-up rider at many rodeos, riding alongside the bronc riders and bull riders and helping them to safety after they'd completed their eight seconds.

'That was the plan, but, you know,' he paused thoughtfully and scratched the chestnut tail, 'I played with some cattle on him yesterday, and he was cutting them like a pro. I've never felt anything like it. He just did it naturally. I was thinking of having a go at cutting.'

Those words, spoken aloud for the first time, set in motion a new future for Brandon. His journey along the path of rodeo sports, of roping and bull riding, switched, and he was now heading down a new road.

Amy dreamed of riding for her country over the famed three day event courses of the world. It was something that burned in her heart for as long as she could remember, and a similar dream involving cutting suddenly blossomed in Brandon's chest as he spoke the words. He wouldn't just 'have a go' at cutting; he and Nu-man would set records that would have crowds on their feet stomping and applauding across Australia and then in the United States.

'So, are we going to stand around and have a mothers'

club meeting here,' Brandon looked around at his friends, 'or should we head straight out so we can spend the rest of the day setting up camp?'

'Whatever you want,' Mrs. Winter told them. 'I have lunch almost ready if you want to have it here, or you can get going and have it at your new home for the next four days.'

They were all keen to get going. Dane started the truck to warm it up, and they dropped the tailgate of the gooseneck so they could load their horses.

'Did you want to put Nu-man on the gooseneck with our fellas or take Gertrude out?' Dane asked Brandon.

'He may as well stay on the float, and I'll bring Gertie out,' Brandon spoke in his slow, drawling voice that often gave people the impression that he wasn't smart. Everyone who knew him well realized that he had a first-class mind. His intention of becoming a veterinary surgeon was not an empty hope, and he had the grades at school to get him there.

'At least that will give us a run-around vehicle,' said Lani. 'The truck can stay hooked up to the gooseneck, and we'll unhook Gertie and use her to get around.'

'You just want an excuse to drive my gorgeous girl, don't you, Lani?' he teased her.

'I'd like to drive her off a cliff,' Lani shot back as they walked across the grass of the quadrangle to the stables.

'We might need to do that to get her going,' he laughed. 'She started OK early this morning when I hooked up the float. Then it took twenty minutes to get her going the second time. Cow of a thing.'

'Battery?' asked Dane.

'Assault and battery, more likely,' he grinned. 'The battery was charged - she didn't want to go. She does that all the time these days – one good start a day and then nothing. So, I hit her around the motor with a spanner until she went.'

'He's joking,' Lani explained to Amy. 'No one can fix engines like Brandon.'

Brandon looked embarrassed about the compliment and changed the conversation, turning to Amy, 'Which horse are you taking?'

Amy had been quiet while most of the bantering took place, feeling like the outsider as her cousins and Brandon refreshed their lifelong friendship. On the bus trip home, she had become comfortable enough in his presence to join in with the light-hearted chatter, but she couldn't quite get into the swing of it now. She thought of things to say and realized, before she uttered them, that they would sound lame in the dancing conversation the others kept up, so she remained quiet.

'Days, the palomino,' she said quietly, picking up a headstall and lead from the pile sitting on a drum outside the stables. She wished she could come up with something funny to add that would have them laughing.

'Nice horse,' Brandon nodded. He had seen her ride him at the Pony Club gymkhana at the end of the last holidays. 'I Googled him while I was at school. There were some great photos of you and him jumping on the Horse Deals gallery.'

Lani cut in enthusiastically, saving Amy from the difficulty of answering, 'He is totally over-the-top wickedly awesome. Amy let me put him over some jumps yesterday, and I fell in love with him.'

They caught their horses and led them back to the gooseneck while Lani continued her story about jumping Days, and Brandon occasionally teased her with a smart comment. The Winters led their three horses, Misty, Fleet, and Shandy, to the truck. Days, at sixteen hands, towered over them.

'So, of course, I love Fleet more than any horse in the world,' said Lani as she finished the story of putting Days over the show jumps and led her grey horse up the ramp into the gooseneck, 'but while I was riding Days I felt like I was in heaven – honestly, that horse can jump like nothing on earth.'

'Have you got some toilet paper?' Brandon asked her when she shut the divider on Fleet and stepped out to let Matthew lead Shandy up.

'In the front of the gooseneck,' she told him without seeing the trap he'd set. 'Why?'

'That verbal diarrhea you have has left something on your chin that you need to wipe off.'

Matthew and Dane burst into laughter. Lani gave him a whack on the arm before succumbing to the giggles with Amy.

'I'm a bit excited, alright?' she challenged him. 'So, I talk a bit much when I'm excited, but riding Days was great, and now we're all going out camping by ourselves. These are big things. We used to think it was pretty impressive just camping in the stables or the garden – but this,' she shook a finger at him, 'this is our biggest adventure ever.'

'So, get that big yellow horse on board,' Brandon grinned at Amy as Dane shut Misty in her bay, 'and let's get going.'

'Can I go with you?' Matthew asked Brandon as they shut the gooseneck with the four horses safely on board.

'Sure thing, buddy,' Brandon agreed. 'Climb into Gertie and push my stuff onto the floor. It won't fall any further once it's there.'

'You stay safe tonight,' Mrs. Winter told them, giving each a quick hug. 'I'll be out tomorrow morning to make sure everything's OK. If you're worried, come home, or call on the two-way and I can come and get you.'

'We'll be fine, Mum,' Matthew assured her. 'We're not babies anymore.'

'You'll always be my babies,' she smiled, trying to stop her eyes from filling with tears. It only seemed like yesterday that they were in prams, and then little Brandon was coming over to stay, and he and Dane played with toys in the sandpit. Before she knew it, they were doing primary school by distance education, and then they were away at boarding school. Now, they were driving themselves out to camp for four nights.

She didn't want to be over-protective, but sometimes it was hard letting them grow up when every part of her wanted to keep them safe and close. Losing Geoff had been the most challenging time of her life. They had been best friends as well as husband and wife. They had done everything together, always with a laugh. His death made everything else so difficult, and the fear of losing others she loved hung over every thought she had about the children.

But what could go wrong? They weren't even leaving Sunhaven. They were merely heading out to the end of the hills to camp. She shivered as though something walked over her grave. I'll go out early tomorrow morning to check on them, she told herself, and I'll call them on the radio this afternoon and tonight, just in case.

Dane climbed up into the driver's seat of the truck. Lani and Amy clambered in next to him, and Blaze jumped up to sit on Amy's lap before she placed him in the space behind the seats. With a wave to Mrs. Winter, he shifted gear and moved away slowly, giving the horses plenty of time to adjust to the motion. Once the truck and gooseneck had started gaining speed on the dirt road heading away from the house, Brandon followed in his old ute, Gertie. A couple of failed starts had meant he had to climb out and use a tool to tap the starter motor before she spluttered into life. Matthew sat next to him, prattling away, one hand waving absently at his mother.

They were on their way to the greatest adventure of their lives so far – to look for the Min Min lights.

*****

Getting Closer

Jake rubbed his hands down the sides of his jeans impatiently as he watched Skinner and Meat throw stones at a tree trunk. They had spent a few days at a remote stretch of the Corona Creek north of Quilpie, and he was keen to get traveling again. He hadn't heard any radio reports about people finding a body back near Lake Bindegolly, so he figured they were still flying below the police radar in Queensland. The cops were still looking in New South Wales and Victoria for them. They should keep moving.

'Let's pack up and get goin',' he called to them.

They stopped and turned to look at him. Skinner shrugged, 'Yeah, whatever. Where we headed this time?'

They walked over to Jake as he lay out the maps Jess had bought for them, and he pointed at their position, 'That's us. We're going to have to head up into Longreach to cross the Thomson then go towards Winton and decide whether we take the main road up through Mt Isa or take back roads straight across to the border.'

'Will we make Winton by tonight?' Skinner eyed the map dubiously; he'd never been good at reading them.

'We could,' nodded Jake, 'but I thought we'd pull up on the Thomson tonight somewhere, then get off the main drag and go bush again, taking the back roads through this country.'

His hand traced a line below the road between

Longreach and Winton, sweeping over various station names, including Sunhaven Downs.

Meat shrugged, 'I just want to get into a town and have a burger. Can we get that in Longreach?'

'Sure thing,' said Jake. 'Camp cooking not good enough for you?'

'Nuthin' beats a burger,' Meat nodded.

'Then we'll stop in Longreach for them, camp out the other side, and head to Winton after that. We'll be in the Territory before you know it.'

Jake folded the map with the rectangle showing Longreach, Winton, and Sunhaven Downs uppermost.

HORSES OF THE LIGHT

CHAPTER FOUR
The Cry of the Min Min

Dane parked the truck near a small stand of gidyea trees about twenty meters from a windmill near the northern end of the Sunhaven Hills. It was only a short ride to the opening of the narrow gorge, which split the hills in two from end to end. A creek bed, dry except for some deeper water holes, wound its way out of the ravine and past their campsite before twisting across the plains country, the taller trees marking its path across the grass and gidyea tree flats.

The windmill pumped bore water out of the ground from one hundred meters beneath the surface and into a large tank and troughs for those times when the creek was dry. Although there was water there at present, the cattle enjoyed the slightly salty bore water, and their dusty trails led to the troughs from all sides, like highways leading into a city. A patch of deep green mimosa bushes huddled near the windmill, and the bright cheeping of hundreds of zebra finches punctuated the hot morning air as they darted around the thorny branches.

Brandon parked the old Gertie at a right angle to the gooseneck so that they had a protected area between the two vehicles, and they began the job of setting up their campsite. They unloaded the horses and tied them to the truck while they erected the yards. There were enough trees in the clump of gidyea to act as fence posts for the electric fencing they had brought, running the tape from tree to tree to make several yards. They also set up the portable steel yards under the trees, which ensured that all the horses had shade during the day. Dane ran a hose from the bore water tank to the yards so that the water could gravitate to their containers and save them the effort of carting buckets of water. Once every yard had feed and water, they untied the horses and led them over.

They struggled to pull out the awning from the gooseneck, collapsing in laughter as they realized they had no idea what they were doing. Finally, Amy made the sensible move of reading the instructions that came with the unit. Once they raised it according to the instructions, they organized the table, chairs, and barbeque to become an outdoor living area. Blaze lay in the shade watching their activity, his tongue lolling out as he kept himself as cool as possible. Now and then, he trotted over to Amy for a pat and then returned to the shade.

'Fridge is working OK,' Amy called out from inside the living quarters, 'and the water is pumping.'

The solar panels on top of the gooseneck provided power for those electrical items. They would start the generator when extra power was needed for the air conditioner, microwave, and kettle. They hauled the generator out to a spot about twenty meters away so the noise wouldn't disturb them too much, and Dane started it to give everything a test run.

Matthew clicked the air conditioner on and sighed, a

smile on his face as the breeze chilled him. 'Ah, that's better. You guys go outside and put something on the barbeque for lunch, and I'll make sure this keeps on working.'

The air conditioner stopped as Lani switched off the power and unplugged it. 'Forget it,' she told him dryly. 'You're not lounging around here while we're outside working.'

'Aw, Larns,' he complained as he made his way outside. 'It's like a million degrees outside today. I think there's a Workplace Health and Safety issue here – I should be allowed to cool down under the air conditioning.'

'Help us finish the last of the setting up, and we'll all go for a swim in the gorge in about half an hour.'

'Sounds fair,' Matthew cheered up instantly. He bounced down the steps of the gooseneck to continue organizing their campsite, his concerns about the heat suddenly forgotten with the prospect of a swim in Sunhaven Gorge.

'I think that's about it,' announced Lani, standing hands on hips as she gazed around at their home for the next four nights. 'It sure beats sleeping on the ground in swags.'

'By about a million percent,' Brandon grinned. 'I can't get over having a proper bathroom out here; I mean, this rig has everything.'

'It is great, isn't it?' Amy still found it difficult to believe that her aunt had given this to her. She felt it was too much for just riding for help on that night when Uncle Geoff died, but it didn't seem so bad having it if she shared it with her cousins and friends.

'It'll be like our own house tonight,' Lani patted the side of the gooseneck and smiled at the boys, 'and Amy and I will sleep like babies up in the comfy beds while you lot toss and turn in the back section.'

'There won't be much sleeping tonight,' Dane promised, 'we'll be looking around the gorge, remember? It'll be torches, cameras, videos, and action for the first night of looking for the Min Min.'

'Yeah, yeah, yeah,' Matthew screwed up his nose at his brother and waved his hand at him imperiously. 'We've been over it a zillion times: night one, we explore the gorge looking for the Min Min. Night two, we look around the bottom of the hills down this end because Uncle John said he saw them here twice. And so on, and so on. We know all that. But that's tonight, big bro – now it's the middle of the day, and it's stinking hot. Let's take the horses over to the Gorge. It's so hot, and they'll want a swim, too.'

'That's got my vote,' said Brandon.

'How deep is the water?' asked Amy, wondering if they could swim or only splash around in a shallow pool.

'Deep,' Dane held a hand well over his head, 'and cold. The water in the gorge is freezing.'

'You turn blue.' Lani shuddered at the thought. 'I mean, you literally turn blue with cold.'

'It's awesome,' laughed Matthew. 'You freeze your monkeys off and then sunbake like a big ol' lizard on a rock to warm back up.'

'Freeze your monkeys?' Amy questioned him, her green eyes sparkling with amusement. 'Do I even want to know what you mean by that?'

'Not really,' he grinned cheekily. 'I just made it up 'cause it was a bit more polite than what I could have said.'

Dane gave his brother a gentle shove towards the tack box. 'Well, you and your monkeys better get headstalls for our horses while I give Mum a call on the two-way to let her know all's good. Then we can get a move on.'

They buckled headstalls on their horses and looped the lead ropes around, tying them so that they could act as reins. Even though Days was sixteen hands, Amy had no problem vaulting onto his back. Reaching up to take a handful of his white mane in her left hand, she rocked back onto her left foot and sprung off the ground, landing in the perfect position for riding.

Brandon whistled, 'Impressive! I'm fine with Nu-man,' he paused as he vaulted on to the broad Quarter Horse back, 'but I don't think I'd make it up on Days quite so easily.'

'She did gymnastics,' Lani told him as she guided Fleet past him, heading towards the gorge. She was proud of her cousin's achievements and abilities and wasn't above giving Brandon a hint that Amy was a girl he should seriously admire. Also, she wasn't completely blind to the shyness that seemed to overtake Amy in his presence. She guessed that her cousin had begun to find the wild rodeo boy attractive, which he was, she thought, but he was too much like a brother for her heart to dance to the tune of his good looks and movie star smile. 'Amy can somersault in the air. She can walk along and bounce, and then she's flipping over in the air and lands back on her feet. It's amazing.'

'I don't do it all the time,' Amy laughed. Lani had made it sound like it was just a normal part of her walk, like a limp. 'It's not like I walk down the street and start leaping into the air and tumbling.'

Brandon's deep blue eyes gleamed as he regarded the girl on the big palomino. She was so like his friend Lani to look at, and yet different in subtle ways. He knew if he insulted Lani, she'd hit him, but he was worried about saying anything that would upset Amy because if she didn't realize he was teasing, she might feel hurt. He might look like someone who couldn't see past his rodeos and horses, but underneath the swagger and joking, he was sensitive to the welfare of others.

'I think you should do at least one tumbling pass down the main street of Winton,' he grinned at Amy, 'just make sure we're all there with the video so we can catch the action.'

'If I could do it, I'd leap around doing it all the time,' said Matthew, imagining himself walking down the main street of Winton or Longreach doing a mid-air tumble every few steps. 'That would be the coolest thing ever. Hey, are you guys only going to walk to the gorge?' he squeezed Shandy's sides, and the chestnut lifted into a canter. 'I'll get there first!'

The others urged their horses into a canter, and Blaze ran at the heels of Days. They all rode as though glued to their horses' backs, their bodies moving in partnership with the movement of the horses. Matthew steered Shandy over a log that was only half a meter high. The other four followed, laughing as their horses jumped into the air, their souls singing at the freedom of being young and on the backs of horses they loved in the heart of Australia. They allowed the horses to accelerate into a fast canter, and they let out yips and cries of pure joy as they raced over the grassy tussocks to the gorge. They were home in the outback on their horses, and life was beautiful.

It was only a few minutes to the six-bar gate in the fence that kept the stock away from the Sunhaven Hills and less than a minute from that to the first of the water holes at the opening of the gorge. A small circle of clear water reflected the surroundings of sandbanks, large flat rocks, and eucalypts. Amy thought it looked like the scenes many artists painted of the outback, with the red cliffs of the gorge rearing up on either side, the intense colors of the trees and sand, and the stark contrast between the brightness of everything in sunlight and the depth of the purple shadows. It was almost fifty meters from one side of the canyon to the other across the rocks and sand, but Amy knew that the gorge narrowed in the center of the hills until it was only four meters across. That was the narrow point that she jumped Laddie over on the night of the storm.

Matthew rode Shandy into the water and laughed as the chestnut pounded his front legs until water erupted over them in great splashes. 'No, don't you roll!' he shrieked at Shandy as he began buckling at the knees to lie down. 'Get up, get up!'

Shandy reluctantly walked out of the water and shook himself so violently that Matthew almost tumbled to the ground.

'You're trying to kill me!' he accused his horse.

Lani rolled her eyes at his dramatics, 'Sure, Matty, he's plotting to take over the world, starting with shaking you off into some soft sand.'

He grinned, 'You think you're joking, but, I'm telling you, he's a smart horse.'

'Not too smart - he's still carrying you,' Dane pointed out as he rode on past the waterhole.

'Our spot is another few hundred meters in,' Lani told Amy.

'But this looks perfect,' Amy looked around at the little piece of Eden.

'It gets better – I promise you,' she said over her shoulder as Fleet broke into a trot along the canyon floor.

They rode single file as some of the huge boulders only left room for one horse at a time to pass. The canyon began to grow cooler as it narrowed, with less surface area exposed to the sun's warming rays. They fell silent as they rode. There was something of the quality of a church in the tall sides and stained glass window colors, and all the children felt a sense of reverence for this special place as they gazed around at the perfect mix of water, rock, trees, and sky.

Sand and grass muffled the horses' hoof steps. Occasionally, they crossed over large flat slabs of sandstone, and the clip-clopping sounds echoed loudly off the cliff sides until it sounded as though a hundred horses must be approaching down the gorge. A couple of times, they halted and listened to the few seconds of echoing hoof falls, turning to each other to smile at the sound.

'It's like there are ghost horses in here with us,' Amy marveled.

'Maybe that's why everyone says that the gorge is haunted,' Lani suggested, her green eyes bright with wonder. 'It's not that the Min Min live here; it's just that the walls make these phantasmagorical echoes, so it sounds like there are others here.'

'Hell-oooo!' Matthew shouted up the canyon as they sat still on their horses.

The greeting returned again and again as the sound waves bounced off the walls, twists, and turns of Sunhaven Gorge.

Cupping his hands on either side of his mouth, Dane shouted, 'Hell-oooo the Min Min!'

The sound of his call distorted and came back at them in layers until the words 'Min Min' distorted into a strange humming sound.

They looked at each other in surprise. Brandon shouted out, 'Min Min', and they listened, fascinated, as the two short words bounced around until the sound became an unusual throbbing *mun-mun-mun-mun* coming back down the gorge at them.

'That is so cool!' exclaimed Matthew, wide-eyed. 'It sounds like a didgeridoo.'

A high-pitched wailing chased the echoes down the

canyon walls at them, sending chills up their spines. The horses threw their heads high and stared up the gorge. They shuffled nervously as though they wanted to turn tail and race back out onto the open plains. Blaze jumped in front of Amy and Days with his hackles up. A deep-throated growl came out of him as he glared in the direction of the noise.

'It's just a bird,' Dane laughed hollowly, 'or something like that.'

'Yeah,' Brandon agreed half-heartedly, trying to reassure the others as much as himself. 'Probably just a curlew. They make weird noises.'

The unusual ground-nesting bird did make eerie calls, but they all knew that the cries came during the night. Amy had first heard the bush stone-curlews at boarding school in Brisbane these past months. She had been frightened by the peculiar haunting sounds in the middle of the night until Lani explained they were from a bird. Some people claimed that the sound was the dead calling for all that they had lost. Amy could understand that claim when she lay in bed in her dormitory at school, listening to the sad wailing of the curlews in the night.

'Yep, a curlew.' Matthew nodded with quick, nervous movements.

'OK, I'll accept that it's a curlew.' Amy looked from one to the other, her eyes narrowing as she weighed her words, 'as long as you all stay here with me. If I'm here alone, I'm thinking that those sounds are from the Min Min, and they're coming to get me.'

'Agreed,' grinned Dane and Brandon together.

'So, let's keep going.' Lani clicked Fleet up into a trot along the sandy stretch ahead of them. She looked back over her shoulder and admonished the boys, 'And no more calling up the Min Min, OK?'

They trotted silently, listening to the echoes of the hooves, and lost in their thoughts about that noise. After a few bends, the canyon narrowed even further, and the waterholes joined up into a running creek with sparkling clear water. Springs in the heart of Sunhaven Hills fed the watercourse, and it ran even in the longest of droughts. As the water approached either end of the gorge, it went underground, so it was only when it rained that the creeks flowed out of the ends of the hills.

'There's our place,' Dane announced, checking Misty with a barely perceptible lift of the reins. 'If the Min Min lights do live here, it's because this is the closest thing to heaven that you could find anywhere. We call it the Sun Pools.'

All the horses halted. The five outback riders drank in the scene for several minutes. It was only thirty meters from wall to wall, with the canyon floor carpeted in green grass that had a lawn-like appearance from the kangaroos that trimmed it back with their grazing. The midday sun was directly overhead, so the entire floor glowed with sunlight. The sun lit the gorge brilliantly, amplifying the colors to a dreamlike intensity. A ledge of orange sandstone almost a meter-high ran from side to side, and the water cascaded down the center of it into a series of rock pools that were clear and inviting. The closest pool had a sandy bottom; the rest were in smooth rock.

Dane pointed to a coil of white electric tape on a tree at one side of the gorge, about fifty meters from the natural rock barrier. He explained to Amy, 'We can let the horses go once we put that up – they won't try to jump up that ledge to go further into the gorge, and they can graze here and play in the sandy pool if they want. We'll swim in the rock pools.'

'It is unbelievable,' she breathed, trying to take in the

beauty of the scene. 'I mean, it looks magical.'

'I haven't been here since last summer,' Brandon looked around. 'I'd forgotten how it hits you. Magical...' he considered Amy's impression of the scene. 'I guess it is.'

'This is the best time of the day,' Lani pointed at the sun overhead. 'The sunlight makes everything glow. The shadows will start to grow in the next hour, and everything changes. At night it looks pretty spooky.'

'Enough of the spooky,' Matthew slid off Shandy and went to the electric tape so that he could set up the temporary barrier to keep their horses with them. 'Let's just enjoy the sunshine.'

They set up two strands of electric tape across the gorge and released the horses. It made an effective fence even without a power source as the horses respected the biting zap of electricity that it usually contained. Shandy headed straight into the sandy pool to complete the process of lying down in the water that Matthew had stopped at the first waterhole. The other horses set about grazing on the lush carpet of grass. Blaze bounced into the water and began swimming around, yipping at the ripples he was creating.

The Winters, Amy, and Brandon ran straight into the first large rock pool in their t-shirts and shorts. They spent the next hour swimming and playing under the waterfall, frequently climbing out of the cold water to warm themselves in the sunlight before jumping back in with exclamations about the freezing temperature of the water. Amy wondered how the water could be so cold in summer in the middle of the outback, and Lani pointed out that it only had sunlight on it for a few hours in the middle of the day. For the rest of the day, the cold rock of the gorge protected it, so it was always far cooler than on the plains.

When dark shadows from the western wall of the gorge

crept across the waterholes and began climbing the eastern wall, they knew it was time to go back to their camp. The brilliant light gave way to a softer glow that reflected off the red walls of the eastern cliffs where the sunlight still hit. Their laughter and voices echoed happily around the canyon, but they remained aware of the eerie cry that had chilled them and alarmed the horses when they arrived. As the light left, so, too, were they keen to leave.

They caught their horses, took down the white tape, and carefully rolled it up. Mounting, they turned the horses' heads for their camp. Riding out of the gorge, they chattered about all manner of things but carefully avoided the subject of that cry. They were determined to accept that it had been a bird call.

With the horses back in their yards, they took turns to have quick showers in the gooseneck. They changed into clean, dry shorts and t-shirts and sat down in the shade to plan the rest of the day.

'I'll give Mum another call in a while, so she knows we're OK. I know she's going to be worried sick about us,' said Lani.

'And I'm going to make us some sandwiches,' said Matthew, who was proud of his sandwich-making ability. 'A plate of mixed sandwiches which will keep Mum happy about healthy eating, but we'll have junk food with it, so all the bases are covered.'

'We probably should try and have a sleep this afternoon if we can,' Dane suggested. 'We're going to be up most of the night looking for the Min Min.'

'So, we're going back into the gorge tonight?' Amy asked him, a slightly worried half-smile on her lips.

Dane gave her a reassuring look. 'There's no difference between day and night, apart from the lack of light and the fact that the Min Min only seem to get seen at night. There are no ghosts or vampires lurking around, waiting to come out at night.'

'The Min Min might be lurking around, and how do we know they're not ghosts or vampires?' she raised her brows at him.

'Because ghosts and vampires aren't real, and the Min Min are,' he countered.

'But if they're real, maybe they are ghosts, and that would make ghosts real, wouldn't it?'

'You think too much.' Brandon grinned at her and softened his words with a wink that made her catch her breath. 'No one has ever been found out here with vampire bite marks on their neck. I'm sure anyone who's ever disappeared probably had reason to, and it had nothing to do with the Min Min. And they helped you that night, didn't they?'

Amy remembered feeling lost on the top of the hills with the rain so heavy that it shrouded everything, and she couldn't find her way. She remembered the desolation of knowing her Uncle Geoff, Aunt Eleanor, and Matthew could be dying after their car accident, and she was the only hope of getting help to them, but she was lost. Then the strange lights had shown up and, believing they may have been walkers with torches, she followed them, but it soon became apparent that the unearthly lights guiding her down unknown paths to Uncle John's homestead could only be the Min Min. They jumped from one place to another in an instant and floated between the trees in a way no person with a torch could imitate.

There was no doubt they had helped her that night and, though nothing could have saved Uncle Geoff, she managed to raise the alarm and have a helicopter fly in to rescue her aunt and cousin. They could have led her off a cliff in the dark as she and Laddie would have followed them blindly, but they had led her carefully down the safe path to the homestead below.

'I guess they aren't going to harm us,' she conceded, 'but what if they feel we're threatening them? They might not be safe if they think we're invading their territory.'

Brandon tapped his temple with a finger and silently mouthed, 'Don't think so much.'

She shone him a smile that caused him to blush under his tan.

Dane and Matthew were blind to the interchange, but Lani smiled to herself when she saw it. It made sense, she told herself as she looked from one to the other; they both loved horses, they both had problems in their family backgrounds, both were really smart and had big ambitions. In fact, she looked from one to the other, pursing her lips in thought, she couldn't think of a more perfect match than Amy and Brandon. Knowing them as well as she did, she realized it could be years before they worked that out for themselves.

'So, let's catch some sleep now while it's still hot,' continued Dane, 'I think we can spare the fuel to run the air conditioner for a few hours so we'll be comfortable. Then we can have a look around, have dinner, and head out on our search.'

When Dane started the generator, Amy switched the air conditioner on so that the gooseneck was cooler than the oppressive heat of the outdoors. Amy and Lani climbed up into their sleeping area and watched a movie about horses while Blaze lay flat out on the floor, pleased to be out of the heat. The boys lay in their bunks in the back section, watching another movie on a portable DVD player. They didn't notice when they fell asleep. One by one, they drifted into the land of slumber as the air conditioner's hum provided white noise in the background.

*****

Closer Still

'Just set the tent up anywhere here,' Jake instructed the other two as they looked around the site near the banks of the Thomson River, near Longreach, to camp for the night, 'I don't think anyone is likely to come along.'

Meat ran a finger across his throat, 'And if they do…'

'Whatever,' Jake shrugged. 'I want to get this trip over with so we can sleep in proper beds. I'm getting sick of sleeping on the ground.'

'Wanna keep driving tonight?' Skinner asked him.

Jake shook his head, 'Nah, the car is beginning to overheat. I want to have a good look at it before we go on.'

As Skinner and Meat erected the tent, Jake looked under the car's bonnet and fiddled with a few things. It was developing problems, but he thought he could nurse it through to the Territory. He didn't want to attract attention by stealing a car at this stage, though he wished he'd taken nosey Bob's car back at Lake Bindegolly. Still, it would only be a matter of time before Bob's family would be searching for that car, and no one was looking for this one which Jess had bought and registered in her sister's name, so he thought he had probably made the right decision.

As the late afternoon ticked away, Jake examined the detailed maps of the area. He looked for tracks through properties so they could turn off the main road. He wrote directions and distances down on a scrap of paper to help navigate the outback.

15 km then turn left; 6 km then right; cross creek keep going another 12 km; Sunhaven Hills on left.

He paused for a moment, looking at the homesteads on either side of the long stretch of hills, but he wanted to avoid houses if possible. He intended to skirt around the northern end of the hills by mid-morning and follow the dirt tracks to enter Winton from the south. From there, they would head out the Kennedy Development Road to Middleton and up to McKinlay. It was longer than sticking to the Landsborough Highway, but it would keep them off most main roads.

If the car played up too much, he'd have to see about picking up a vehicle from one of the stations along the way. He eyed the twin dots on either side of the Sunhaven Hills. One of those places would be likely to have a car that they could take. If there were people home, they'd deal with that at the time. Meat was always keen to kill, but the more bodies they left behind, the bigger the hunt for them would become. He would have to keep Meat under control.

****

'They said they're headed north and then into the Territory,' Bob struggled to talk to the police officer who had found him by Lake Bindegolly.

'Just rest, mate,' the policeman told him. 'The ambulance isn't far behind me.'

'I'll be fine,' Bob assured him. 'My wife always said I had a thick skull. You need to put out a warning on those blokes. Dangerous men. Three of them. They had prison tattoos.'

He shut his eyes for a moment, and the young officer thought he'd lost him, but he was resting. Bob had spent days lapsing in and out of consciousness lying under his car in the shade, crawling to the lake's edge to drink water and cool himself down when he could.

When he realized that the men had disabled his car, he decided to wait with it because he could not risk trying to walk out while disoriented with a concussion. He had some biscuits which Jake had missed, and he knew those, along with the water, would keep him alive until help arrived. He knew that it would only be a day or two before his family would send out a call for help, and then a search plane or helicopter would locate his car, so he needed to wait with it.

He had heard the plane buzz overhead that morning and return within a minute to make a lower pass over the clearing where his car was parked. The pilot, he knew, would recognize the large X he had made on the ground next to his car using branches as the international symbol for 'require medical assistance.' He was right. The pilot radioed back about finding the car and the signal for help and called for the police and ambulance.

'You've got to stop them before they hurt anyone else,' Bob told the officer.

The distant wailing of the ambulance grew louder.

'Three men with prison tattoos?' the younger man checked with him. 'Driving a four-wheel drive like yours and heading north then to the Territory?'

Bob nodded.

'Any names?'

'I forget,' Bob shrugged then grabbed at his head in pain, 'but they had lots of tatts on them, the sort they get in prison.'

The clues fell into place, and the police officer was sure he knew who the men were. They were looking for them in New South Wales and Victoria, but it seemed the killers were crossing outback Queensland. They were probably in the Territory by now, but every police officer in the outback of Queensland needed to be on the alert for these men, and people needed warnings about how dangerous they were.

HORSES OF THE LIGHT

CHAPTER FIVE
The Galaxy Walk

'We've had a good day so far,' Lani spoke on the radio in the front of the truck, 'we're going to have tea and then go for a walk in the moonlight.'

She took her finger off the button on the side of the mouthpiece and waited for Mrs. Winter to reply.

'Don't stay out too late, and make sure you give a call if anything worries you.'

'Lani worries me!' Matthew yelled from the open door as he saw his sister press the button to speak again. 'What can you do about her?'

He ducked and laughed as Lani swung at him, thumping her hand into the seat where his hand had been a split second earlier.

'Sorry, Mum,' Lani continued, her eyes on her younger brother, who stood a few meters from the truck grinning at her. 'I think Matthew had too much sugar today, and little boys can't handle their sugar.'

Matthew pulled a face at her.

'If you tease each other too much, I'll have to come out

and sort things out,' Mrs. Winter threatened.

'Just joshing,' Lani answered as soon as the static indicated that her mother was no longer talking. 'Everything's good here. We swam at the Sun Pools today.'

'How did Amy like them?'

'She loved them. Who wouldn't? We thought we heard a curlew call out while we were there; it was the weirdest sound.'

'Probably just the Min Min,' her mother said. 'Your Uncle John always swears they live in the canyon.

'Do they make noise? I thought they were just lights.'

'Who would know what they do?' Mrs. Winter laughed. 'I've never seen them. Amy is one of the lucky few.'

'It would be pretty creepy if they made that noise today. We're hoping to see them tonight when we go for a walk.'

'Take a photo if you do, but it isn't likely. Just be careful. The snakes are active at this time of year. Don't go anywhere without the basic first aid kit.'

'Will do, Mum. We'll see you in the morning.'

'I'll be there after breakfast. Love you.'

'Love you more,' Lani smiled as they ran through the script she had used with her mother since she could talk.

'Love you twice as much.'

'Love you, infinitely.'

'Love you double infinity, and over and out.'

The radio went silent.

'Dinner's ready!' Brandon called. 'I have slaved over a hot stove; I've put my heart and soul into this meal, so come and get it and you'd better enjoy it.'

Everyone had a joke about his hot stove remark since he'd served up some cold meat and potato salad out of the fridge. Their good-humored teasing continued through dinner. They sat at the table under the annex, with Blaze at Amy's feet gazing at her as she ate.

'You know he's just trying to psych you into giving him some of your food,' Brandon told her, smiling at the Kelpie at her feet.

'And it works,' replied Amy, handing the dog a small piece of cold roast beef. 'I can feel him sending me pictures of him eating my food, and I just make his wishes come true.'

'You know you shouldn't reward begging behavior,' Matthew told her as he handed Blaze a piece of meat from his plate. 'It's really bad for them. Creates bad manners.'

'Thank you, Mr. Dog Whisperer,' Amy nudged his leg with her foot and grinned at him. 'I hope you'll write a book on dog training so I can get Blaze to read it one day.'

'I might just do that,' he feigned a thoughtful look, 'right after I've written a book on how witty my cousin is... oh, hang on, that only needs two words: she's not.'

'That's pretty good,' Amy conceded, not offended by his teasing as she had learned to give out as good as she received with her cousins. 'You might be able to write a book if it only had two words.'

'Alright, children,' Lani interrupted, 'enough of that – as funny as it is – because it's dark, and we need to hurry up and go looking for the mysterious lights.' She paused and then put on a fair imitation of David Attenborough's voice, 'In the distant outback of Australia on dark and lonely nights, the local children have been known to go looking for the Min Min.'

'That is so good!' Amy exclaimed. 'We have to use that for the introduction to our video.'

'Matthew does the best David Attenborough,' Lani waved a hand at her younger brother, 'and he loves being the center of attention, so I vote that he is our presenter.'

'Yes!' Matthew punched the air, 'I'm in! Hurry up and finish eating, and let's get the camcorder out so I can win an Oscar.'

They finished their meal and, while Dane and Brandon cleaned the dishes, Amy, Lani, and Matthew practiced the introduction to their Min Min video, quickly coming up with a script for Matthew to use. When they were all ready, Matthew crouched in the truck's headlights next to a large tussock of grass and morphed himself into a young Attenborough as Amy filmed. It took a couple of attempts before he managed to get through without mistakes - and without the others bursting into giggles - but the result was worth it.

'Here, in the wilds of Australia,' he uttered his words in the distinctive British tones of the famous documentary maker and presenter, 'we're following the exploits of a group of young locals as they set out on an adventure to find the Min Min lights. The lights of the Min Min are reputed to have been in the area for many hundreds of years, but there's been no scientific evidence to prove that they exist.'

Amy stopped the camera a few seconds after Matthew ceased talking. She had made films at her school in Melbourne and knew to continue the filming for several seconds after the required point to make it easier for editing.

'Remember, Matthew,' she told him in her best director's voice, 'when you stop, keep looking at the camera and count to four slowly; otherwise, you end up stopping and looking away immediately, and it makes it hard to cut it into the next scene. So, finish talking, freeze, and count to four before doing anything else.'

'Got it,' he gave her a thumbs up to show her he understood. 'So, what do we do next?'

'How about Dane and I take some torches out on the flat,' suggested Brandon, 'and we make them look like Min

Min lights as Matty says something about them being rare or no one knowing when they're going to appear.'

'Good idea,' enthused Lani, unable to control her laughter at the thought of the scene, 'and Matthew can rabbit on without being aware they are there spying on him.'

They set the scene up carefully, going over the lines, and then filmed it with Matthew standing in the beam of the headlights. Over his shoulder, the twin lights of the fake Min Min danced in the darkness. Again, it took a few times to have it right as Lani and Amy couldn't stop giggling at the expressions on Matthew's face as he pretended to be unaware of the lights behind him.

'They've never been captured on film before, but these young adventurers are hoping to change that over the next few days. Said to resemble a set of headlights floating in the sky, the Min Min lights remain one of the most elusive phenomena in the world today. Let us follow their journey to discover the Min Min.' He stopped, stared at the camera while he counted to four, and then gave in to the fit of laughter that he'd been battling to contain.

They shot a few more scenes that were difficult to complete without laughter, but their antics put them in high spirits for their first night of searching for the Min Min. They walked to the canyon, still joking about things that made them laugh, their torches in their pockets because the moon was bright enough to light their way. The moon, just a few nights short of being full, flooded the plains with soft light, and the stars, which usually blazed so brilliantly, were dimmed by her glow. Although the bright colors of daylight were absent, it was still easy to make out everything around them, from rocks at their feet to the ancient, eroded sides of the hills with all their shadows and dark places.

Their plan involved going as far into the Sunhaven Gorge as they could in two hours and then coming back out, filming anything of interest along the way. They walked and jogged the short distance to the hills, which took about fifteen minutes, then they each took a deep breath and pretended to the others that they weren't scared and stepped into the canyon entrance. Once they entered the gorge, they followed the same path they had taken on their horses earlier that day, using their torches to check their footing as the moonlight didn't reach the sandy floor to reveal the treacherous rocky outcrops. With their torches lighting the way, they made fast progress along the canyon floor.

Their voices and laughter became more subdued as they traveled, as though they did not want to disturb whatever lived in the gorge. By the time they reached the Sun Pools, they had fallen silent, and the mood of lightness evaporated, replaced by a sense of anxiety about being in the dark in the place where the Min Min lived. Making plans to find them had been so exciting on the bus and at the Sunhaven Homestead with Mrs. Winter a shout away, but now it seemed a little frightening. Amy was glad to have Blaze at her side as she hoped he would protect them if they needed it.

They stopped at the Sun Pools and stood for a few minutes, shoulder to shoulder, regarding the water. The moon was now high enough to cast her light on the water, and the small waterfall danced in the light, sending bright ripples radiating out across the first pool. By the time the water reached the last of the round pools, the surface was as still as a mirror. The sound of the running water bounced around the walls of the canyon, and though they strained to listen for other noises, there were none. No crickets. No birds. Just the sound of water and nothing else.

'You know,' Brandon broke the peace with a whispered voice, 'if that curlew cries out again, I'm going to be running out of here as fast as these cowboy legs can carry me.'

'Nah, mate,' Dane shook his head and grinned at him, 'if that happens, you'll be lying in the sand because I'll have pushed you down and run over the top of you to get out of here.'

'What about me?' Matthew looked from one to the other of the taller, older boys.

'Sorry, bro,' Dane shook his head. 'I'm feeling so on edge right now that if something goes boo in the night or that curlew calls, you're on your own.'

'We'll be here for you,' Amy told him.

'Speak for yourself,' Lani snorted. 'If that bird calls out with that cry of the dead, I'll be trampling everyone to get out of here first.'

They all chuckled softly at her words, but the ability to laugh out loud seemed to have withered in the cool night air of Sunhaven Gorge.

'Do you think it was a curlew?' Matthew asked, gazing up the canyon from where the sound had come earlier that day.

'What else could it be?' Dane shrugged, trying to convince himself with his words as much as his brother. 'No one has ever said the Min Min made noises. They're just lights. Probably swamp gas.'

'Probably,' Brandon nodded, as though agreeing, and then smiled at them all, his eyes resting for a moment on Amy's face as the moonlight played on her features, then he continued. 'But if we believed that, would we have bothered with this trip? Come on, admit it, we all think they're something more than that. Ghosts, creatures of the

Dreamtime, maybe even aliens. We haven't said what we really think, but we know they are *something*.'

'So, we keep going?' Matthew kept his voice low, like the others.

Amy broke rank and began walking towards the rock shelf that ran across the width of the gorge. 'We keep going. For another hour, at least.'

'I'm with you,' Brandon said as he strode after her. 'Just keep in mind, I wasn't joking when I said I'm out of here if that bird wails.'

'Chicken,' Lani teased him, knowing full well that Brandon was one of the bravest people she'd ever known. She had seen him stand up to boys far older and bigger to protect a victim of their bullying. If ever she had to be in a situation that involved danger, he was someone she'd want beside her. Although he joked about it, he would never run and leave a friend behind.

'Better a live chicken than a deep-fried eagle,' he grinned, knowing how ludicrous his words sounded.

'Don't think I've ever heard of Kentucky Fried Eagle,' Dane pointed out as he followed the others up over the ledge and deeper into the gorge.

'You might get to eat deep-fried curlew, though,' said Brandon, now walking beside Amy as they followed a clear trail along the floor of the canyon. 'I'm telling you, the sound of those birds creeps me out.'

'Nice birds, though,' Lani added, 'I like how they freeze if you get near them, believing that if they are still, you won't see them. You know if you harmed one, I'd have to drop you as my friend, Brandon Suffolk.'

'Is that how I get rid of you?' he turned to look at her, his eyes wide. 'Just hurt a defenseless bird, and then fourteen years of friendship is over?'

'I'm thirteen,' she pointed out.

'I was visiting Sunhaven when you were inside your Mummy's tummy,' he put on the voice of someone speaking to a young child, 'so I knew you before you were born.'

Lani gave a splutter of laughter, 'And you were a few months old… good memory, there, Brandon.'

'I have a photogenic memory,' he deliberately used the wrong word, causing the others to snicker softly. They understood his humor and knew it amused him to substitute the wrong word. Some people made the mistake of assuming he was not very bright.

They walked on for several minutes in silence. Brandon and Amy led, with Blaze an arm's length in front of them. Lani and Matthew followed, and Dane brought up the rear. With the moon overhead, they didn't need their torches to see the path. They followed it as it wound between the rocks and trees alongside the small creek that flowed across the rock pools and sandy floor.

'What made this path?' Amy turned her head to look up at Brandon.

He looked down at her and smiled softly, 'Worried the Min Min made it?'

She shook her head, 'It's just that I know the cattle and sheep are fenced out of here, so it's not from their hooves.'

'Kangaroos and goats,' he told her. 'I'm surprised we haven't seen any or heard them. The hills are filled with them. There's probably a thousand goats living in the Sunhaven Hills, and they're often down here in the gorge.'

'I want a baby goat,' Matthew piped up from behind them. 'If we see one, can we get it?'

'That would be a kid,' corrected Lani.

'I'm too young to have kids,' Matthew grinned at her. 'I just want a baby goat.'

'You are a baby goat,' Lani prodded him gently in the

ribs, 'and, no, you can't have one. I am not going to take a baby away from its mother, breaking their hearts, so that you can have a pet. If we find one that has lost its mother, you can have that one.'

'Fair enough,' he shrugged, then looked around and stopped. 'Hey, does anyone else have a funny feeling?'

They all stopped and looked at him.

'Funny as in ha-ha, or funny as in weird?' Lani asked.

He searched the dark walls of the canyon, and ahead at the moonlit strip of sand and rocks along the bottom of the gorge, 'Funny, as in someone is watching us…like there's something in the shadows.'

'OK, officially feeling creeped out,' Lani raised her hands. 'I didn't feel it before, but now I do.'

'There's nothing,' Dane assured them, 'Matthew just felt something, and it's his words that have you feeling funny, Lani, just his words. Nothing is watching us.'

Matthew squared up to his brother, 'Hang on a minute - we're here because we believe the Min Min might live here, and I think something is watching us, and you say it's nothing. You can't know that. You know I'm nearly always right when I say someone is watching.'

'So, do we go on?' Dane checked with the group. 'Or is it getting too scary, and we should turn back?'

Amy gave a slight shrug, 'He only said he felt something was watching, not that something was going to attack. It could just be some kangaroos watching, couldn't it?'

'Could be,' Matthew agreed.

'So, let's keep going,' she continued. 'When we reach our turn-back point, we'll do a bit of filming, have a snack and a drink, and then head back.'

'And don't break into a run,' warned Lani. 'You know what it's like if you're outside at night and head back to the house at a walk, and it's all OK, but if you start to run, panic sets in, and you bolt. So, we walk out, the same as we came in.'

'Agreed,' Brandon said as the others nodded. 'Stay calm at all times, no matter what happens.'

Blaze halted and stared into the darkness of the canyon ahead, his hackles up, growling softly.

Patting the dog to soothe him, Brandon repeated, 'No matter what happens.' He looked around at the others, making sure that Blaze hadn't unnerved them.

They started walking again, each now conscious of Blaze's wary walk and occasional low growl, as well as Matthew's sense of being watched. They all knew that he was rarely wrong when he reported that feeling and they found themselves staring harder into the shadows. They strained to hear any noises apart from the echoed sounds of their voices, their footsteps, and the soft tones of running water.

The moon moved across the sky, beyond the western rim of the canyon wall so that they could no longer see it, and the light was creeping up the eastern wall with darkness chasing it. They went back to relying on their torches to find their way between the rocks and over the patches of lawn-like grass, which made areas of the gorge seem like tended gardens. A slight breeze picked up and moved down the gap, gently touching their faces as they walked into it, rustling the leaves on the trees around them.

'Nearly time to call it a night,' Dane murmured to the others as they crossed another lawn.

'Has anyone else wondered where all the animals are that keep this grass mowed like a bowling green?' Lani frowned as she looked at the grass beneath her feet in the beam of the torch. 'I haven't seen a kangaroo or wallaby or anything. Something is keeping this grass trimmed short, but where are the animals?'

'Maybe we scared them out of the gorge today when we were swimming,' suggested Amy, 'our voices would have echoed along the length of it.'

'Yeah, that'll be it,' Matthew nodded, still unable to shake the sensation that prickled up the back of his neck, telling him that they were being watched. 'I think we're just getting a bit jumpy. We should have explored here during daylight.'

'Scared, little bro?' Dane patted him on the back, not teasing, just asking.

'No one's seen the Min Min in the day,' Matthew pointed out sensibly, 'so I know we had to come here at night, but, you've got to admit, it is pretty disturbing here.'

'Yeah, it is,' Dane nodded. He was beginning to sense a presence around them that he couldn't define, just a feeling deep inside that they weren't alone in the gorge. 'I think it's time to have Matty do some more Attenborough stuff and then skedaddle out of here and get some sleep.'

Laughter burst out of Brandon, 'Skedaddle? Really, Dane? Skedaddle?'

'Hey, I think it's a beaut word,' Dane defended his vocabulary.

'Yeah, for our great grandfathers,' Brandon teased him, then repeated the word a couple more times to feel it roll off his tongue. 'You know, you're right – it is a pretty good word. I think I'll start using it now. I am officially adding skedaddle to my list of words describing speed and motion.'

'Would that make us skedaddlers?' Lani asked, enjoying the bantering as it took her mind off the unease about being out at night with unknown things in the shadows.

'Yesterday we skedaddled,' Amy joined in, putting on her best school teacher's voice, 'today we skedaddle, tomorrow we will be skedaddling. We are the skedaddlers.'

'Love it!' Lani laughed, then her amusement dried up as she pointed, 'Look!'

They had rounded a small bend in the gorge, now only twenty meters wide, and ahead of them, the walls sparkled in the torchlight as though ten million stars shone from the rock. They stopped and stared, awed by the beauty of the twin walls of reflected lights. They stretched up to meet the sky where stars blazed down on their earthly counterparts. The torchlight was broken up and repeated so many times that the narrow canyon glowed with light.

'Wow!' Amy murmured, 'That is amazing.' She felt an unaccountable desire to burst into tears as the magnificence of the sight made her feel emotional, as though... she fumbled for the thoughts that eluded her. It was as though it didn't belong in her world.

'It's the Galaxy Walk,' Dane informed her. 'There's crystal in the rock here. This is what happens at night when torchlight hits it.' He shone his torch over it, and the beam fragmented into a million tiny reflections. 'It's even more impressive at sunset. There's a layer of crystal across the eastern wall near the top, and the last bit of sunshine hits it at just the right angle to make the light explode out of the crystal. It throws the light down the canyon walls like a waterfall of gold for about five or ten minutes, and then it's gone. It's amazing. We should come back tomorrow to see it.'

'It sounds incredible,' Amy shook her head, her eyes wide as she gazed at the sparkling canyon cliffs.

'It's a piece of heaven,' Lani told her gently in a voice that showed reverence for the sight. 'When we were little, our grandmother brought us here and told us that, according to the legends, this is the entrance to the Dreamtime. It is the gateway to heaven. She said that when people died, their souls came here to find their way to the stars.'

Tears began to roll down Lani's cheeks as she looked at the stairway to heaven and wondered if their father's soul had come here the night he died. Did their Nanna climb down from heaven, following the stars, to meet their dad and take him back with her?

'I don't think Dad would leave us,' said Matthew, his eyes looking up at the stars in the small patch of sky atop the Galaxy Walk. 'If he came here and saw the stairway to heaven, he'd have turned away so he could stay with us.'

Dane laid a light arm across his brother's shoulders and gave him a quick squeeze, 'Maybe that's who's watching us now, eh, Matty? Maybe Dad can get to heaven through here as Nanna said, but maybe he can climb back down from the stars when he needs to see us.'

Wiping his cheeks with the back of his hand, Matthew nodded.

'The gateway to heaven,' Amy whispered, half to herself, 'do you think my Dad could come here even though he died overseas? Can the angels come back down from heaven?'

'I don't know,' Dane sighed, wanting to believe the legends but knowing that they were looking at crystal fragments in rock, not a portal to another world. 'They're just stories, words made up about a place that looks like it doesn't belong in our world. I think we have to hold the people we love in our hearts, not expect to see them come back to us.'

Amy nodded, realizing the sense of his words, 'Perhaps it's more like a church than a gateway – a place to remember the ones we've lost, not a place where we'll meet them again.'

Brandon sighed, thinking of his family members who had passed away, 'Smart words. How about we stop here, take a few minutes to look around, film Matthew doing his thing, and then head back to our beds.'

They agreed and drifted apart, each with private thoughts of loved ones they'd lost and each with tears in their eyes which they wanted to hide. The fears that hovered around them as they walked through the gorge seemed to evaporate in this magical place. Settlers called it the stairway to heaven when they found it over a hundred years ago. For thousands of years before that, the original custodians of the land named it the path to the Dreamtime. This was not a place to be scared, and they had no qualms moving apart from each other.

Amy walked between the crystal-encrusted walls with her torch switched off as the others provided more than enough light to make the tiny pieces of crystal glow like cities spread out over the rock. She wondered about the crystals' light and if there was any connection between them and the Min Min lights. If those ghostly lights that flashed between the trees to guide her down the hills some months earlier lived anywhere, she thought, this would be it: lights living in a place of light.

Lani, Dane, Matthew, and Brandon turned their torches off, and the walls caught the moon's beams which touched them at the top. The moonlight bounced around and cascaded down the crystals until it filled the canyon with an ethereal glow. The five of them stood in silent wonder at the sight, their heads back gazing heavenwards. No one had words to describe the moment, but they looked at each other and saw that they all felt it.

'I don't think I want to film here,' Amy shook her head slowly, trying to explain how she felt. 'I want to protect this place, not put it up on YouTube so that people will see it and want to come here.'

Lani was glad that Amy had voiced that opinion. 'I

agree. I don't think many locals know about the Galaxy, much less people outside the area, and I think we should keep it that way.'

'Fine by me,' Brandon agreed. 'I've only seen it once before, and something about it made me keep it a secret. Maybe your Nanna told me to keep quiet about it - I don't know. I know I wouldn't like strangers hiking in here to look at it and chip away bits of the walls to take away with them.'

'Let's go back around that last bend and do some filming there,' suggested Dane.

They began making their way back down the gorge but, before they left the sight of the crystal lights behind, Amy took one last look back and asked something that had been playing on all their minds.

'Why do I feel safe here in this light when I was having the socks scared off me for the last hour?'

Brandon looked at her, the soft light of the Galaxy Walk highlighting her fine features, and he felt a sudden, almost physical pain in his chest. 'It could just be the light. Until now, shadows filled the gorge. Here, the crystals in the walls have destroyed all the shadows and throw the light everywhere. Well, that's a logical explanation, and it makes sense. Most people are scared of shadows at night.'

He finished with a shrug, not fully believing his own words. It was not just the light that made him feel safe here; there was a sense of well-being, as though someone was standing guard over him, keeping him protected. He guessed that the others experienced the same sensation, but he did not want to put forward that notion when a common-sense one was the most likely explanation. Even Blaze was wagging his tail as he sniffed around, his earlier wariness forgotten in this place.

They filmed their next segment out of sight of the

Galaxy Walk, their torches supplying the only light apart from the line of moonlight high up the canyon wall. The shadows crowded around them, held at bay by the torches and the light on the camera. Matthew continued his remarkable impersonation of David Attenborough as he explained that the locals claimed the Min Min lights resided in this area, waving his hands around convincingly.

'Could that be the elusive Min Min lights now?' he asked the camera dramatically, peering back over his shoulder. Two lights approached him through the dark, but as they neared, Dane turned both torches, one in each hand, onto his face and grinned happily.

'Just one of the local ruffians having a joke,' Matthew continued, then froze and counted to four as Amy had instructed him.

'That'll do for tonight,' Dane yawned. 'I want to hit the sack and get some sleep.'

'That's right by me,' Brandon nodded, catching the yawn.

They packed up and walked back out of the canyon, feeling the presence that had disturbed them earlier but refusing to admit to the others what each felt. Their torch lights cut thin lines through the shadows as they lit the path for their own feet, and they kept their eyes down so that they did not trip over anything. No one noticed the two lights that hovered far behind them near the top of the canyon walls, watching over them.

*****

'Fixed the car?' Skinner asked Jake as he leaned over the motor and peered in. His torch pointed at the jumble of engine parts that was a mystery to him. It was close to midnight, and Meat snored in the tent behind them.

'It'll do,' Jake sniffed and wiped an oily hand across his

face. 'We'll get another if it lets us down.'

'Not many cars out here,' Skinner eyed the massive black emptiness that surrounded them. He had been born and raised in city limits and had never seen the night without the glow of street lights and urban sprawl. It wasn't to his liking, but life inside a prison cell was even less enjoyable, so he handled the outback without much complaining.

'There's enough,' Jake spoke curtly, 'we can get one easy, any time.'

'If you say so,' Skinner did not want to argue with him, 'I'm turnin' in. What time we gettin' up in the morning?'

'Not too early. I want us to be through Winton by lunch, and it'll only take three, maybe four, hours the way I've planned, staying off the main road. We'll make those Sunhaven Hills late morning and then shoot through to Winton.'

While Skinner crawled into his swag, Jake stayed up longer, leaning on the car and looking at the moonlit landscape. His father had brought him out this way several times when he was a boy. Those had been the only happy memories in his childhood of abuse and suffering. His parents separated before he was born, and his mother had raised him with less care than a spider for her offspring. There was a blur of memories: seeing his mother drunk or unconscious from drugs; a never-ending march of men in and out of his life who hit him, yelled, and forced their nightmares on him.

He learned you were the bully, or you were bullied. While he was young and small, he was bullied by all around him except for those occasions when his father swept into his life to take him on a trip. As a ten and eleven-year-old, he practiced day after day with a knife at the back of his mother's shed until he could throw it accurately into a target at ten meters. His knife was his protector, and he made it clear to his mother's friends that he would use it if they raised a hand to him.

With cunning brought about by the desperate struggle to survive in a violent home, he told them that he could kill them and he would escape punishment because he could convince anyone that it was self-defense. If they harmed him, how would anyone believe that a man was defending himself against a child? He scared them. By age twelve, he learned that once men feared you, they tended to leave you alone. At school, the lessons learned at home brought him trouble. He ran away from both home and school when he was thirteen and lived on the streets.

Life was not a pleasant journey for Jake. The roads he traveled and choices he made led to jail, where his kill-or-be-killed philosophy kept him at the top of the pecking order. There was no kindness, no safe place to call home, no memories of happiness apart from those distant trips with his father through the outback. If he was capable of loving anything, it was this land. Here he felt free. He wanted to reach the heart of his country, somewhere in the Northern Territory, maybe in the Ord River region, and find refuge.

First, he had to reach his destination, and the reliability of their vehicle was doubtful. Still, he shrugged to the stars; if he had to steal one, he would.

******

Bob's message about the three criminals finally made it on to the news for the midnight bulletin. Police suspected the three escaped criminals were traveling through the outback, headed towards the Northern Territory, possibly via Longreach, but they could be anywhere. They warned people to treat them with extreme caution and not to approach them as they were considered armed and dangerous. Descriptions of the men and their vehicle were issued, and listeners were urged to immediately report any sightings to police. They were the three most wanted men in Australia, and details of their violent crimes repeatedly played on television. The radio news issued urgent updates asking people to report any suspicious activity or sightings.

CHAPTER SIX
The Calm Before the Storm

The sun rose on clear skies and quickly began heating the land. The gooseneck door and tailgate were open so that the night air could circulate and keep the temperature down to make for comfortable sleep, but the glaring light of morning was difficult to sleep through. During the night, Blaze had left the floor and found a spot next to Amy's legs where he could stretch out next to his human. When she woke, she felt his weight pinning the sheet down.

'Ugh,' she groaned and pulled the sheet out from under the dog who thumped the bed a couple of times with his tail to let her know he was awake. 'You are a total lump, Blaze, do you know that?'

The tail thumped a bit faster in reply.

'I *thought* he climbed up here during the night,' Lani pulled a face at the Kelpie who still hadn't moved, apart from the wagging tail. 'You are a spoiled dog, do you know that, Blaze?'

'You awake?' Dane called from the back section.

'No, just talking in our sleep,' Lani replied, smirking at Amy over the silly question, which deserved a silly answer.

'I'll have bacon and eggs for breakfast, then,' he requested, knowing full well the nature of the answer they would fling back at him.

'Me too!' Brandon and Matthew called in unison, having a chuckle at the three seconds of simmering silence that greeted their teasing.

'You can take a flying leap,' Lani barked at them.

'Aw, come on, Larns,' Matthew wheedled, 'I really want my bacon and eggs.'

'And in which universe do we cook breakfast for you?' Lani asked. 'It sure isn't this one.'

'We'll do breakfast if you make the chocolate milk,' Dane offered after some quiet negotiations with Matthew and Brandon. They knew the girls would be happy with a bowl of cereal each, but they wanted a cooked breakfast.

'Deal,' replied Amy, 'and we get first go at the bathroom.'

'Only if you're quick,' said Dane, 'no half-hour beauty treatments or anything.'

'Oh, sure, Dane,' Lani shook her head at Amy and rolled her eyes, 'and since when do you see us do that sort of thing?'

'I don't know what you do behind closed doors in the bathroom,' he grinned at the other two boys, 'and I don't want to know.'

'But if it's a beauty treatment,' added Matthew, 'it isn't working.'

The boys cackled and didn't hear Lani's smart rejoinder about them needing veterinary treatment. The boys cooked breakfast on the barbeque outside when they finished laughing while Amy and Lani organized drinks.

Stepping out of the gooseneck with a tray of cups in her

hands, Amy announced, 'Choccy milks all round, although I don't get why we want to have hot chocolate on a hot morning.'

'Habit,' shrugged Dane, 'we've just always had it when we're home.'

'That's a good enough reason for me,' said Amy, handing him a mug.

'What time do you reckon Mum will come and visit?' Matthew asked as he served up some bacon onto the plates Brandon held out for him.

'I reckon,' Brandon closed his eyes for a moment as though in deep concentration, 'in about seventy-five seconds.'

They looked at him, puzzled by the precise time. He nodded in the direction of the homestead, and they turned to see the dust plume approaching.

'She's missing her babies,' Brandon grinned at them, 'like a mother hen coming to check on her little chickees.'

'Yeah, well, don't forget Mum counts you as one of her little chickens,' Lani told him dryly, 'though I think you might be the ugly duckling.'

'So, going to grow into a beautiful swan, eh?' he raised his brows at Lani and put the bacon-laden plates down on the table for everyone.

'No, you're more the ugly duckling who's going to grow into the ugly duck,' she smirked at him.

He put a hand to his chest and feigned an expression of pain, 'I'm wounded.'

Lani laughed at him, 'I'm not fooled, Brandon, I know that *you* know you're not an ugly duckling - more the fancy rooster who drives all the girls crazy. Except for Amy and me, of course.'

Amy became suddenly busy pouring cereal into a bowl, her head down so that her hair fell across her eyes and shielded her from Brandon's sharp gaze. She wondered for a moment about the girls Lani mentioned with her *all the girls* phrase. Amy had never thought much about boys before because she had been so obsessed with her horses, and she certainly wasn't thinking about Brandon as a boyfriend now, she told herself, but she couldn't help speculating for just a second or two. She wasn't going to make a fool of herself, though, she determined as she added milk to the cereal; if *all the girls* were going crazy over him, she didn't want to be just one more.

'Mum's here!' announced Dane, oblivious to the undercurrents between his best friend and his cousin.

The four-wheel-drive pulled up near their camp, and they lined up to welcome Mrs. Winter to their home away from home, offering her breakfast and showing her around their campsite. With appropriate comments of admiration, Mrs. Winter gave her seal of approval and felt a lot more at ease about them camping out without an adult. Everything was sensibly and safely set up, and it seemed as though they were being practical about spending a few days away from the homestead.

After breakfast, they walked down to the creek and looked around for seashells which, Mrs. Winter informed them, had been deposited there millions of years ago when the sea covered all of inland Australia. It was close to lunchtime before she headed back to her vehicle, satisfied that they were no more likely to run into trouble here than if they'd set up a tent in the backyard. She reminded herself that boys Brandon's and Dane's age had once lied about being older and run off to war. Her grandfather had left home at fourteen and gone to work with strangers a thousand miles away from home. They could look after themselves.

Still, it was difficult to leave them.

Mrs. Winter looked over them, 'I heard on the radio this morning that police think three escaped prisoners are driving through the outback, and they're quite dangerous.'

Dane gave her a wry smile, 'We heard that too, Mum, but we're not too worried. The outback is a big place. They could be two or even three thousand kilometers from here and still be in the outback, so having them turn up here is a needle-in-the-haystack chance.'

'I know, but it's my job to worry about you.'

'Don't worry so much, Mum,' Lani hugged her, 'we'll call you if anything goes wrong, or we'll pack up and come home. We have our horses - nothing's going to go wrong while we have our horses.'

Mrs. Winter scanned the clear skies. No storms in sight. All was well. And yet, an uneasy sense of...she searched for the source of the feeling. It was as though a storm was approaching, but there were no storms. She shrugged to herself. She didn't like the feeling of her babies growing up and becoming independent.

'I know, I know,' she smiled at her children, counting her niece and Brandon among her brood, 'it's just a mother thing.'

'No, it's not,' Amy shook her head, a gentle look on her face as she regarded her aunt, 'I don't think my mum worried a day in her life about me. She'd drop me off at horse riding camp, forget to pick me up three days later, and then say she didn't realize I'd been away. It's not a mother thing, Auntie Eleanor; it's an Eleanor Winter thing.'

'I agree,' nodded Brandon, thinking of his mother who did not show much care about his whereabouts or well-being, 'but it's nice to know you worry about us, Mrs. Double-you.'

Eleanor gave Brandon and Amy a quick hug, feeling the

years of pain that lay behind their words. No child should have to think that their mother did not love them above all else, and it pained her to think of these two young people growing up with feelings of abandonment. As she'd done earlier, she looked from one to the other and realized that they were perfect for each other… in about ten years, her motherly internal voice added. It wouldn't do for them to start having romantic thoughts about each other at this age.

'We'll be all right,' Matthew held open the car door for his mother and spoke to her like a parent trying to placate a child. 'We survived last night, and we'll survive two more days and nights, and then we'll see you again – nothing's going to happen. And we'll call you on the radio tonight or tomorrow morning, and we'll call you if anything does happen, but it's not going to.'

'Make it tomorrow,' she told him, giving the top of his head a quick rub, amused by how he tried to ease her worries with his old man routine. 'I'm going over to March's place for a baby shower after lunch and probably won't get home till midnight. I might even stay over if you're sure you won't need me. Uncle John has gone into Winton for some meetings today and tomorrow, so if you need someone, well, I guess you'll have to call March's or drive over to Marantha Station to see the Winfields.'

After she left, Amy gazed at the dust cloud kicked up by the car. As she watched the red cloud drifting slowly across the paddocks, she suddenly felt very vulnerable, out here in the middle of nowhere without an adult, looking for lights that were reputed to abduct people who followed them. They had helped her the night she jumped Legend's Leap, but would they always be so benign, or could they steal souls as some claimed? They were real, she knew that, but what exactly were they? And did they truly want to come face to face with the Min Min lights?

Despite the heat, a shiver ran down her spine, and she wrapped her arms around herself defensively. Something bad was going to happen. She knew it. They should stop looking for the Min Min lights and go home and hope never to see them again. Some mysteries were better left alone.

'You OK?' Brandon spoke softly from beside her.

Amy jumped. She hadn't noticed that he had walked to her side. 'Yeah,' she smiled up at him, putting her fanciful thoughts away, 'I just think we should go for a ride before we lose any more of the day.'

'Agreed,' he winked at her in that disarming way that made her feel as though they were sharing a secret when she knew it was just how he charmed everyone, and he did it without thinking. 'I want to have a look around the base of the hills for an hour or so. There are some good jumps there for you and Days if you want to get airborne.'

'Sounds good,' she danced away from him, heading back to the gooseneck to change into riding clothes, unaware that his gaze remained on her as she left.

After changing out of shorts and into jeans, they put their saddles out and went to catch their horses, bringing them back to the gooseneck to brush them, clean their hooves out, and saddle up. Amy and Lani both rode in all-purpose English saddles, though Amy kept her dressage and jumping saddles in the tack box for eventing. Their bridles were plain leather snaffles with cavessons across the nose, and they both had sparkly crystals in the browbands because they liked the bling. Dane and Matthew rode in Barcoo stock saddles and used stock bridles with big loose-ringed snaffle bits, while Brandon had a western swinging fender saddle, which he used at the rodeos, and a snug-fitting snaffle bridle with a kind bit.

'I gather you're not going to be doing any jumping,'

Amy eyed the two stock saddles and the western saddle, all built for flatwork as the shape limited the rider's ability to adopt a good jumping position.

'You girls are cleared for take-off,' Brandon grinned at them, 'but we'll be sticking to the ground today. Give me the comfort of this beauty over those little racing pads any day.'

They knew he rode in an English saddle for certain events at the shows and pony club, but Amy had to admit he looked far more at home in the western saddle than he did in the all-purpose she saw him use at the gymkhana in the last holidays. He was a born cowboy.

After leading their horses around a few steps to check that everything was fitting properly and no girths were pinching, they mounted and headed towards the hills at a walk. The care of their horses was the foundation of their riding, and walking to warm them up at the beginning of a ride and again at the end of the ride to cool them down was something they practiced without thinking. To them, seeing someone saddle up a horse and canter off was a clear sign of inexperience and lack of care for the horse.

They walked for a few minutes then pushed their horses up into a trot. Days swept ahead with his huge scopey trot, each stride covering almost twice the distance of the other horses. Now and then, Amy would slow him down to let the others catch up, then let him power away again.

'I love his trot,' Lani told her when Amy slowed Days back again to ride alongside Fleet. 'I wouldn't swap the Fleetster for anything in the world,' she reached down to pat his neck and admire his grey ears that flicked around to let her know he was giving her his attention, 'but Days is the sort of horse every girl dreams of if you know what I mean.'

Amy nodded, 'Yeah, I know what you mean. He was

my dream horse. He gave me some great rides in eventing, but I think showjumping is his favorite. He could go to the top in jumping as he can launch himself over anything even though he's not as big as some of the horses out there, but for three day eventing,' she paused and shrugged, 'I don't think he has what it takes to get to something like the Olympics or WEGs. I could be wrong, but he feels tired at the end of the cross country.'

Competing at the World Equestrian Games had long been one of Amy's dreams, though now that she had the right horse, she saw it as an ambition, not just a dream. From the first moment she had seen Laddie, the big chestnut gelding that had carried her over the massive gap of Legend's Leap, she had felt in her heart that he was the horse that could handle the toughest three day event courses in the world. He had the attitude of a horse that would kill the cross country course and pull up exhilarated rather than exhausted. He had the movement of a dressage horse and the courage required of a jumper. Every part of her believed that Laddie would carry her to victory.

'You know you'd better have me along strapping for you if you get to the Olympics or WEGs with Laddie,' Lani warned her cousin.

'Don't worry - you'll probably be out there competing in something, too.'

'Fleet isn't up to much more than state-level polocrosse and some local show jumping,' Lani admitted honestly, 'I love this horse to death and trust him with my life, but I know his limitations.'

'Why not try Days at some jumping events and see if you like competing on him? Then you can borrow him if you like. Once I start work on Laddie, I'm not going to have enough time to give him the attention he wants, anyway.'

For an instant, Lani's eyes lit up at the prospect of competing on the big palomino, but then she looked down at the flicking ears in front of her. She wasn't ready to move on from Fleet. He was the friend she turned to when she was sad, the horse who had carried her to hundreds of wins in many different fields of riding. When she needed to be away from other people, she could jump on him bareback and ride away from the house, knowing he would take care of her. As tempting as it was to move on to Days, she could not abandon the horse who had been her faithful companion for so many years.

'Maybe I'll do that one year,' she told her cousin as she gently stroked Fleet's neck, 'but I'll stick to my grey man for a bit longer.'

Amy nodded. She knew how much her cousin loved her horse – how much all her cousins loved their horses. It was obvious that Brandon also had that deep bond with Nu-man that was the mark of a good horseman. The gelding trotted along on a loose rein; his attention split evenly between everything around him and his rider. Amy could see that horse and rider were so in tune that Brandon only had to think canter, and the young horse would stride forward into the right gait, and a mere raise of his hands that didn't even put pressure on the bit was enough to have the horse slow down.

It was good being one of the outback riders, she smiled softly to herself, including Brandon in their group. Maybe one day, they would all compete at international level as they all had the natural talent of great riders. That was a dream worth following, she thought as she sat down in the saddle and asked Days to canter, the outback riders all competing for Australia.

'Jump!' Lani cried, pointing to a log ahead.

The girls headed their horses over it as the boys rode

around it. There were more obstacles as they cantered along around the edge of the hills: fallen logs, part of an old rock wall that marked a long gone cottage, ditch jumps along the edge of the creek, and a nice spread made from a pile of old timber. Days ate up the jumps, and Fleet took everyone bravely, though he had to put in a lot of effort to clear anything much higher than a meter.

'Have a go on Days,' Amy offered her horse as they halted under the shade of a tree to give the horses and Blaze a breather, 'I'll sit here with Fleet, and you put him over the spread, some of those ditches, and those two logs over there that you reckoned were too big for Fleet.'

Quick to take up the chance to ride Days, Lani dismounted and handed her reins to Amy before getting a leg up onto the Palomino's back. Luckily, both girls rode with the same stirrup length, so she could ride off without needing to make any adjustments. She walked and trotted a circle and cantered a figure of eight with a simple change. Then she asked for a flying change and was delighted to feel Days lift and change legs in the air like a skip so that he landed on his other canter diagonal.

'I love this horse,' she shouted to Amy, a laugh in her voice, 'I only had to *think* flying change, and he did it. I have to set Fleet up for at least five strides before a fly, telling him over and over, *get ready for the flying change, get ready for the flying change, and change*. But Days just does it.'

'He'll do two-time changes as easy as anything,' Amy told her, describing the movement that required the horse to change his canter diagonal every two strides, 'he's so light on his feet that he's always ready to skip into another lead if you think it.'

'Well, now he can show me how light he is over the jumps,' Lani turned him towards one of the smaller logs, which he cleared in his canter stride with barely a change in rhythm.

The stack of timber which she had refrained from attempting with Fleet was next in her sights. It was over two meters wide and almost a meter and a half high, and she shortened up Days' reins as she headed him towards it, assessing the length of his strides and judging the distance as she approached so she could have him in the correct position for perfect take off. On Fleet, she would have felt him beginning to hesitate and question the jump in the last three strides, but Days just powered up underneath her and left her with no doubt that he was going to clear it easily.

In that instant of take-off, Lani felt her future rushing at her. Jumping Days was like opening the door to a kaleidoscope of hopes and dreams and possibilities that showered light and color down on her. Fragments of a possible future with fleeting images of show jumps, stadiums, and crowds on their feet applauding flicked through her mind. She had always enjoyed jumping their horses, but this was a whole new level of jumping to their pony club and local show activities. This was perfection, and it was wholeness; it was the most exhilarating feeling she could imagine as they soared through the air over the large pile of cut-down trees in the middle of a paddock in the outback.

After a safe landing, she turned Days back to Amy and Fleet and shook her head. She couldn't go on jumping him. It was like glimpsing paradise only to know that it wasn't hers to have because she had other things to do.

'What about the ditches?' Amy asked her.

Lani dismounted and handed the reins back to her cousin, 'Give me another year with Fleet, and I'll start thinking about Days. If I do any more with him now, I won't want to get back on Fleet, and he's my man,' she rubbed Fleet between his eyes, and he leaned into her, 'so, don't you worry about me moving on from you, Fleety-pie, you're the best horse.'

Once back in the saddles of their horses, the girls cantered after Matthew, Dane, and Brandon, who had ridden on around the edge of the hills. They traveled another couple of kilometers around the northern end of the hills, training their horses as they rode along. Brandon showed the others how to start a proper reining spin by walking progressively smaller circles until his horse planted one hind foot and did a half turn around it, then he was walked out of the circle to maintain forward movement. Amy demonstrated how the walk pirouette was different as the horse was not meant to anchor himself by that inside back hoof but was expected to continue a proper walking pattern as he described a small circle around his hindquarters.

They stopped at a small gully with water in the bottom of it for the horses and dismounted to spell them and eat the lunch they'd brought in their saddlebags. As they sat in the shade munching on vegemite sandwiches, they watched a mob of feral goats climbing the tumbled rocks of the edge of the Sunhaven Hills. Nannies and kids walked and jumped up the ledges, following invisible paths to the eye so that it looked as though they were magically ascending a cliff. Dane explained to Amy that there were thousands of feral goats in the area, descended from the tame ones that people used to keep for milk and meat, and the males, the billy goats, ran in their mobs, leaving the nannies alone until mating season came around.

The midday heat was intense enough to drive the kangaroos to the shade for the day, and they spotted several families sprawled out in the shade of trees not far from the waterhole. Some of the big red males stood up to watch them, and they looked to be well over two meters tall. Their blue flyer mates with the pretty bluish-grey faces relaxed on the ground, trusting that the big reds would warn them if danger threatened.

'I think it's time to turn back to the air conditioner,' Matthew grimaced as he leaned against Shandy, 'it's getting too hot out here for riding.'

'Sooky calf,' Brandon teased him, 'you're getting soft in your old age, Matty.'

'Only thinking of my horse,' Matthew defended his words, 'I can handle it twenty degrees hotter than this, but Shandy is melting.'

'I hate to be a sooky calf, too,' put in Lani, 'but I'm tired after being up half last night, and we have a bigger night ahead of us if we're coming back here tonight to find those Min Min lights. I'm going to head back if you want to join me, Matthew.'

'Want to go back with them, Amy,' Brandon asked her, 'or ride along another few kilometers to see the palm grove?'

'Palm grove?' Amy looked interested, 'I haven't heard of that before.'

'One of the many secrets which Sunhaven will reveal to you over the years,' Dane grinned at her.

'It's where there used to be an outstation,' explained Lani, 'only the cottage burned down decades ago, and all that's left is the garden of palm trees and the orchard around the watering hole so that it sort of looks like an oasis. It is pretty cool, though, and worth seeing.'

'You show Amy the palm grove,' Dane suggested to Brandon, 'and we'll head back to the air-con and get a head start on the afternoon nap.'

'Maybe a sleep would be...' Amy began, only to be cut off by Brandon.

'You can sleep the rest of your life,' he smiled at her

with that winning flash of teeth as he mounted Nu-man. 'Let those wussy Winters go back to the comfort of the gooseneck, and we'll have a look at the orchard. If they're lucky, we'll bring them back some fruit. '

'If there are any mandarins left, I want one,' Lani demanded, 'but it's probably too late for them. What will be there now? Maybe some figs?'

'There's a heap of fruit trees there,' explained Brandon as he motioned for Nu-man to head away from the others. Amy vaulted into Days' saddle and followed as he explained. 'There are springs watering them so that they've survived all the droughts that have been thrown at them since the outstation was abandoned.'

'See you back at the camp in an hour or so,' called Dane as he sat back down on a log next to the waterhole and eyed the water. He lowered his voice to speak to his brother and sister, 'I reckon we should stay here for another ten minutes and look for fish – I swear I saw a big yellow-belly over there under those reeds.'

The three of them stared at the gently swaying reeds on the other bank where soft ripples indicated movement under the water.

'Maybe we can bring back some lines later on,' said Matthew thoughtfully. 'I could handle a big yellow-belly for dinner. Remember when Dad used to bring us fishing along here?'

They were silent for a minute as the memories of their father came flooding painfully back. Sometimes it was easier to not think of him at all than to remember and be hit by the longing for his presence that would never be satisfied. When they did think of him, the memories of his smile and laughter pricked them like needles and brought tears to their eyes. He had taught them to ride, and he'd taken them fishing and camping, he'd carried them on his shoulders and tossed them screaming with laughter into these waterholes; he'd protected them and been there when they needed him.

'Yeah, I remember,' Dane said softly, blinking away the extra moisture in his eyes, 'he said that if he died anywhere in the world, he'd come back to these hills and these waterholes and go on fishing because this was heaven.'

Lani turned away to hide the tears that burned out of her eyes and ran down her cheeks. She missed her father so much. She buried her head into Fleet's mane and breathed deeply. He'd told her that when things were bad, all you had to do was put your face into the mane of a horse you loved and breathe in the essence of horse because, in that, you'd always find strength and peace, no matter how troubled the world became.

A butterfly of the most amazing blue landed on Lani's saddle, and she turned to look at its delicate wings moving gently in the sunshine. She reached her hand out, and it stayed there as she touched it, the wings going up and down ever so slowly. It was beautiful, and she smiled at the wonder of something so perfect sitting there next to her.

'Look!' Matthew breathed as softly and urgently as he could.

Scores and scores of the blue butterflies rose from the reeds and grasses around the waterhole and fluttered past, their sapphire blue colors bejewelling the air. The sadness that had settled on them lifted with the butterflies and soared away.

'Do you think Dad sent them?' Lani asked her brothers.

'Maybe,' Dane shrugged and changed the subject. 'Come on, let's look for fish and then head back to camp.'

He wasn't comfortable talking about their father or wondering where someone's soul might go after death. It made him feel ill to think that perhaps there was nowhere to go, that their father just ended when he died, and all that he was and all the love he had inside for his family and his land vanished into nothingness when his heart stopped beating that night in the storm. He did not want to think about that while Lani stood there, hoping their father was in a place where he could send messages to them in the form of butterflies.

HORSES OF THE LIGHT

CHAPTER SEVEN
Amy and Brandon
1.30 pm - 2.45 pm

'It does look like an oasis!' exclaimed Amy as they rode at a walk around an outcrop of house-sized red rocks and caught sight of the dozens of tall palm trees ahead. She could see other fruit trees scattered around the orchard hidden between the folds of the hills, but the palms caught most of the attention with their tropical tops waving in the breeze.

'Cool, isn't it?' Brandon grinned, admiring one of his favorite spots on Sunhaven, 'I reckon if there were an end-of-the-world disaster that meant we all just had to survive on our own, I'd come here and live. It has everything. Water, fruit, good soil for vegetables, and it's sheltered by the hills.'

'So, this is Brandon's piece of paradise?' she asked him cheekily.

'Yup, that's it. All it needs is a little cabin built under the palms. Don't worry, if the world ever gets too much for you, consider yourself invited to stay here, too,' he glanced at her quickly, a little self-conscious of his words, but Amy's eyes were downcast, so he wasn't even sure she'd heard him. 'Come and check out the trees.'

He clicked Nu-man into a canter, and Days' much bigger stride soon overtook him as they approached the palm grove.

Among the different palm trees were some shorter date palms and ones with white trunks and others that were so tall that Amy thought they must have been growing for more than a century. There were citrus trees, but it was too late in the season for any fruit on them. Behind the trees clustered around the lower parts of the grove, Amy could see a couple of huge, dark-leafed trees with fruit hanging from the branches.

'Oh, you are kidding!' she gasped with excitement, staring at the large, yellow fruits, 'I love mangoes! Look at those mango trees!'

Enjoying seeing her excitement over the discoveries in one of his favorite places, Brandon just nodded.

'And avocados, not that I like them anyway, but bananas – whole bunches of them. I love bananas. And what are those little brown things under that tree?' She pointed to a large tree with a carpet of brown nuts underneath.

'Macadamias. The next crop won't be ready for another few months, but we should find plenty on the ground that are still OK.'

They rode into the shade of the trees and walked around them, trying to work out the identities of the various fruit trees. It seemed ten degrees cooler in the shade of the grove, and small pools of water in various places indicated the presence of the spring water, which kept the trees thriving without human intervention. The grass under the trees was mown into a lawn by the kangaroos that grazed there. Tomato plants, as well as watermelons and rockmelons, rambled wildly in many places. Amy could understand why Brandon would want to build a cabin and live here.

'This must be where Uncle John gets the fruit from when he comes to visit,' said Amy, thinking of him arriving at least once a week with cartons of fresh fruit. 'I just assumed that he had an orchard at his house.'

'This is his garden,' nodded Brandon. 'He puts out the seed for the melons and tomatoes and some of the other things you'll find growing here. It's like a little Garden of Eden. I don't think many people know about it, apart from the Winters and me, and it's well hidden, tucked away in the fold of the hills here.'

'You know, when I first arrived here from Melbourne,' Amy spoke softly as she looked around at the abundance of food growing in the palm grove, 'I thought the outback was just this great big emptiness, but there's so much here. I never realized that the hills would have so much in them with the waterholes, the Galaxy Walk, and now this. Do you think you go on discovering things no matter how long you live here?'

'Definitely,' Brandon inclined his head to look at his horse's mane as he tried to find words for the knowledge that was his heart. 'It's not just about finding new places you've never seen before, though, it's about the storms and the droughts, the good years and floods and fires and starry nights, the sunsets and sunrises and everything that changes from one day to the next. There's always something new. I can't imagine living anywhere else.'

'Don't you want to see the world, though? I want to ride at Badminton and Lexington and take Laddie over some of the great courses in Europe.'

'Have you always wanted to do that?'

'As long as I can remember,' she halted Days and hooked one leg over the pommel of her saddle, trying to explain her dreams to Brandon, who leaned over Nu-man's neck regarding her closely. 'It's something that burns inside me, and I can't imagine what would put it out. I have to do it, no matter what. Isn't there anything you want like that?'

He shook his head slowly, 'I guess I've been too busy getting by. Sometimes it gets a bit tough at home with Mum and Dad... they both drink a bit,' he paused at the understated description of the drunken rages from his childhood, 'but Dad is pretty good. He's always taken me to Pony Club and the rodeos and that sort of thing, and Nan and Pop make sure I have a good education at Scots.'

'But now that you have Nu-man, don't you want to do something great with him?'

'Maybe,' he hesitated then confessed, 'well, funny that you should mention it, but I was only thinking yesterday that he and I should go cutting. I worked some cows with him the other day, and he was like nothing I've ever ridden before, it was...' he took a deep breath, 'it was magic. And yesterday, I had this feeling that we should do that, go cutting.'

Amy noted the light in Brandon's eyes as he spoke of the newly born dream, and she smiled, 'It will burn inside you, and you'll have to do it,' she told him. 'I'll be out eventing, Lani will be showjumping, you will be cutting, and we'll be the world-famous outback riders. We have to find something for Dane and Matty to do.'

'Polocrosse for Dane,' Brandon grinned at her, 'he's already played for the junior state team, and he has his eyes set on the opens. He's obsessed with it if you haven't noticed.'

'Let's get some fruit to take back and come up with a sport for Matthew,' Amy swung her leg back into place and rode to the mango tree to pick a couple of the best-looking fruit.

'Like trick riding or chariot racing. or maybe Ma and Pa plowing competitions?'

Amy burst into laughter, 'That sure sounds like the sort of thing that would appeal to Matty.' She glanced at her watch, 'He'll be getting back to camp soon, getting into bed to have a nap under the air conditioner, and maybe he'll dream up something for himself.'

After collecting some mangos and bananas and stuffing their pockets with macadamia nuts, they began to make their way back to camp. They talked about horses and school and enjoyed the companionable silences as their horses walked side by side, with Nu-man occasionally breaking into a jog to keep pace with the big stride of Days.

HORSES OF THE LIGHT

CHAPTER EIGHT
Jake, Meat, and Skinner
2.00 pm – 3.05 pm

The four-wheel-drive sputtered and surged unevenly, spitting out black smoke from the dying engine. Jake punched the steering wheel savagely and cursed the car that was threatening to strand them in the middle of nowhere. He was angry at himself for thinking the car would get them to Winton or further rather than fixing it in Longreach. He was angry at Meat and Skinner for sitting there morosely, wanting to complain about the situation but keeping their mouths shut because of his foul mood. He was angry at the outback for being so big and so far between service stations and mechanics. He had planned to be at Winton by this time, but they had been forced to stop several times to nurse the car back into life, wasting more than half the day.

'Didn't you say there was a house near those hills?' Skinner asked, pointing at the flat-topped Sunhaven Hills not far ahead of them.

'Yeah, if we can get this heap of rubbish that far,' Jake scowled. 'It should be another ten clicks or so. This road runs between the house and the hills.'

'So, if we can get there, we just take one of their cars?' Meat sniffed.

'These stations usually have a few cars,' Jake told them, remembering staying at several with his dad when he was young, 'and not much security. It'd be better if we didn't have to have a run-in with the people, but if we do, we do, and we'll deal with it.'

A sly smile crept over Meat's face as he imagined meeting with people who might cause them problems, and he clenched his fists. He knew what to do about them, and he enjoyed doing it. He hoped there would be someone who needed his form of dealing.

A flash of reflected sunlight between the trees towards the hills caught Skinner's eye, and he stared, trying to work out what it was. The car shuddered, almost stopped, then lurched forward again, causing another round of swearing from Jake, whose temper had frayed to the point of snapping. Skinner did not want to see him reach that point as he had witnessed it in jail, and it was frightening when the man went off in a rage.

'Is that a house over there?' he asked when Jake finished his cursing. He pointed towards the glint of light between the trees.

Jake narrowed his eyes and tried to make out what Skinner was seeing. It could be a cabin or maybe a caravan. Whatever it was, it was less than a kilometer away, and he was prepared to send the ailing car off the road and over the paddock to find out rather than continue towards the homestead and risk a long walk. He swung the four-wheel-drive off the dirt road, slowed to a crawl, and began to cross the Mitchell grass tussocks towards the gooseneck.

Stopping the car about twenty meters from the gooseneck, Jake surveyed the campsite. It appeared deserted. He narrowed his eyes as he studied the truck and gooseneck and imagined himself traveling the outback in style with that. It was enticing, but he knew they would attract attention in such a recognizable outfit. The old car parked next to it might be a safer bet.

'Do y'reckon anyone's around?' Meat grunted the words as he stepped out of the car and stared around at the quiet scene.

'Don't look to be anyone,' Skinner leaned over his open car door and yawned; this whole outback caper was beginning to bore him. He wanted excitement, not this dull country experience.

'Anyone there?' Meat shouted into the still heat of the morning air.

Silence followed.

'They're out on their horses.' Jake pointed to the empty horse yards and swept his hand around to point to the headstalls at the side of the gooseneck. 'Let's have a look around and see what they've got to offer.'

'Not much,' grumbled Skinner. 'That old car don't look much better than ours. This caravan looks good, but.'

'Gooseneck,' Skinner corrected him, he had worked at a race track for a short time, and he knew a bit about vehicles for carrying horses. 'It's like a caravan and horse truck in one. Living quarters up the front, horses down the back.'

Jake knocked on the door of the gooseneck, waited a few seconds, then opened it and climbed the steps to the interior. Meat followed while Skinner turned to stand guard in case anyone returned while they were inside. Feeling behind him, he checked that his handgun was safely tucked into his belt where he could reach it easily if he needed to use it.

Once inside, Meat swore at the luxuriousness of it; he'd

never seen anything like it before, 'Man, it has everything: fridge, stove, sink, tv, even a shower and toilet!'

'It's a top-of-the-line rig, that's for sure,' Jake agreed as he checked out the beds in the back section where the boys had been sleeping. 'Looks to be four people at least, maybe five, judging by the beds.'

'Ma, Pa an' the kids?' guessed Meat.

'Prob'ly. They might be out mustering. Let's get what we can use, grab that old car, and keep going for now.'

'We gotta take this, though, Jake. We're not taking some shabby rust bucket while this stays here.'

'Think a bit, mate,' Jake tapped the side of his head in a gesture to tell Meat to use his brains, 'you're looking at rig worth maybe two hundred thousand or so with the truck, and it's going to be noticed wherever we go. That old rust bucket will fit in with all the other old cars out there, and no one is going to care so much about it going missing. But this goes missing, and they're gonna come lookin' for it quick smart.'

Meat shrugged, seeing sense in Jake's words, 'Yeah, I guess. So, what'll we take?'

'Food, drinks, anything useful. Let's get it and keep going.'

Jake pulled the pillow covers off to use as sacks, threw one to Meat, and they began opening cupboards and gathering food. There were a few torches, some tins of soft drink from the fridge, and opened some plastic containers with prepared meals in them.

'Tuna casserole,' Meat opened the lid of a plastic dish and sniffed appreciatively. 'Whoever cooked this sure knows how to make it smell good. How 'bouts we wait and take the missus with us as a cook?'

'Yeah, kidnapping,' Jake threw him a sour glance and said sarcastically, 'when we want to stay out of the limelight, that's a good idea, isn't it? Do something that'll have the whole country looking for us. While we're just sneakin' away quietly, we have a chance of running under the police radar, so let's leave the kidnapping alone, eh?'

'Then you probably didn't want me clocking that old geezer back there at the lake,' Meat growled. He thought back to leaving the man lying there, but it meant nothing to him. He had no empathy for other humans. Pain and suffering meant little to him apart from a passing curiosity about how some people carried on about it. 'Maybe I shoulda left him alone.'

Jake bit back the sarcastic retort that almost passed his lips about Meat being a genius but thought better of it. He didn't want the big oaf turning his temper on him.

'Mighta been better if we'd just driven away,' Jake told him calmly, 'but what's done is done, and if we can avoid anything else like that, maybe that would be best, eh?'

Nodding slowly as the idea that not harming others was good for them sank in, Meat agreed to the plan. He did not usually have to think of consequences, he just acted, but he could see what Jake was trying to get at. It was not that the other people were important, but if he wanted to stay out of jail and away from the police, leaving them untouched would be the right action.

'Now, let's get this stuff outa here and see about getting that old bomb going.' Jake had another regretful look around. It sure would be good to cross the outback with this level of comfort, but he was not a stupid man. He knew that they might as well radio police and tell them where they were as take this rig.

'All clear?' Meat asked Skinner as he stepped outside and offered him a biscuit from the Tupperware container he had taken from one of the cupboards, 'Good food, this – take a couple.'

'All clear,' Skinner nodded as he took three of Mrs. Winter's peanut butter cookies. 'We gunna take the old car?'

'Sure thing,' Meat scowled at Brandon's Gertie. 'Can you hotwire it?'

'No need,' Jake told them as he approached the vehicle. 'Out here, most people'll leave their keys in the ignition or under the front seat or on the visor.'

The door squeaked as he opened it and, after a glance at the empty ignition, he pulled down the driver's visor. The keys fell to the seat. He grinned at the others and showed them the keys before putting them in the ignition and trying the engine. Uncharacteristically for Gertie, she started the first time and purred away healthily as though even she feared the men.

'OK, let's load her up,' Jake ordered as he turned off Gertie's engine. 'All our stuff will fit in the back, and the three of us will have to squash in the front. Luckily she's a bench seat and not buckets, so we can fit without breaking the law.'

Snickering, Skinner saw the funny side of Jake's words, 'Nah wouldn't want to break the law.'

'Hey, we pass a police car,' Jake pointed out, 'and we're all legal with seat belts; they probably won't look twice at us. If they pull us over because there's three of us and only two seat belts, then we're done for.'

While Jake made sure Gertie was clear to travel with water in the radiator, adequate fuel and oil, and correct tire pressures, Skinner and Meat began transferring their gear out of their four-wheel-drive. Taking the tool kit he found in the truck, Jake removed the number plates from their old car and threw them in the back of the ute, so they did not make an easy trace to Jessica. He wrote a note to leave at the gooseneck explaining that they were backpackers and were in a hurry to get to Rockhampton, the opposite direction from their route, so borrowed the ute and would send money for it when they could. He hoped that would blow enough smoke over the actual situation, so no one suspected that the escaped criminals had passed this way.

'Hurry up,' he told Skinner as he saw him wander off behind the gooseneck, 'let's get going before they get back from whatever they're doing.'

'Just lookin' around,' Skinner replied, 'you sure we can't take this unit rather than the old bomb?'

'I'm sure, now come on. Let's get outa here.'

'Too late,' Meat shouted at them. 'they're back!'

They looked up to see three children on horses approaching at a canter, angry expressions on their faces, and a total lack of awareness about the situation into which they were riding. Skinner's hand went behind him to rest on the handle of his gun, and he noticed Jake did the same.

HORSES OF THE LIGHT

CHAPTER NINE
Dane, Lani, and Matthew
2.30 pm – 3.10 pm

Dane, Lani, and Matthew had taken their time at the waterhole. The day was hot, and the air that drifted over the water was cooler than anything out in the open paddock, so it made it difficult to ride away. The horses seemed to appreciate standing around in the shade of the trees by the water, as well, their eyes calm and content as they swished flies with their tails and stood with their heads low and relaxed. They had only intended to stay a few minutes, but it was close to three before they decided to move.

'I'm going to end up going to sleep here soon,' Matthew yawned. 'Let's get back to camp so we can knock out some zeds under the air conditioner.'

'Air conditioner,' Lani repeated, a grin on her face, 'now you're talking. OK, let's go.'

They tightened their girths and swung into their saddles, riding their horses up and out of the creek onto the flat country and breaking into a trot as they headed towards the campsite. The horses were eager to get back as they understood that the campsite meant food, and their riders let them break into a canter to eat up the kilometers quickly.

They were still several hundred meters from the camp when they noticed the vehicle parked there. Stopping the horses, they looked at each other questioningly and were able to communicate without words that they had no idea who had dropped in to visit them.

'Maybe one of the jackaroos from down the road,' suggested Dane, with *down the road* meaning anywhere within a hundred or more kilometers. 'We'd better go and see if they need help with something.'

'I don't know the car,' said Lani. 'I heard the Wilsons were getting a new jackaroo this week. Maybe it's him.'

They pushed the horses forward into a canter, their bodies swaying easily with the movement of the horses.

While Dane and Lani talked to each other, Matthew regarded the activity at the campsite where he could see two men, and it suddenly struck him that the back of the ute was loaded up.

'They're stealing Gertie!' he exclaimed, amazed by the fact that anyone would want the old ute.

Dane uttered a curse as he took in the scene and pushed his reins forward to hurry Misty up when he realized the truth of Matthew's words, 'They're not getting away with it.'

'What if...' Lani began voicing her doubts about riding in to confront three unknown men.

Dane cut her off, a strategy forming in his head as he spoke, 'They might take the truck and gooseneck, too, if we don't stop them. We'll tell them our parents are only a few minutes away and scare them off.'

Before she could say anything else, she saw the men

look up to see them and felt fear slash into her heart. These were not the sort of friendly faces she had seen all her life in the outback. Something told her that these men would not be scared off easily by three children on horses telling them that their parents were about to turn up.

'We should go,' she whispered urgently to her brothers, staying stirrup to stirrup with them but urging them to stop and leave, 'turn around and ride away.'

The boys' anger at the intruders was running too high to take any notice of her warning. They were young warriors riding in to defend their territory, and caution fled in the face of the adrenalin rush of riding into battle.

'We're on our horses,' Dane told her, glancing sideways at his sister as they began to slow. 'We're safe. Just don't get off. If they get too close, ride away. As long as we have our horses, we're safe.'

They halted twenty meters from the men and, for the first time, noticed that there was a third one. The men formed a line facing them, the biggest one with a container in his hands, the other two with their hands behind their backs. The door of the gooseneck was open, and the Winters could see the open cupboards and a mess on the floor. It was apparent the men had been rifling through everything, stealing their possessions, and even eating their food. They all recognized their mother's Tupperware biscuit container in the hands of the bulky man.

'This is our stuff,' Dane called to them, his voice that of the brave young warrior who faced his enemies without fear. 'You need to get in your car and get out of here before our parents arrive.'

The man at the center replied, his eyes cold, his body tense as though he was considering springing across the twenty-meter gap between them and ripping them out of their saddles. 'Bit of a problem with that plan, sonny,' Jake smiled without any humor. 'Our car's broke down, and we need to get to the coast real quick. Family emergency, you see. We're just gonna take this old ute of yours, and when we get to the coast, we'll send you some money for it.'

'Not good enough,' Dane's eyes blazed, 'if you need help, there's a radio in the truck – call someone, and we'll get you a lift to town.'

'Nah, I don't think so,' Jake spoke softly, his voice sending chills down Lani's back like ice water. 'We need to go now. You just ride back there and tell your parents that we had to have their car, and we promise we'll send payment for it, or I'll get someone to bring it back to you.'

'Sure,' Dane scoffed, 'like we're going to trust the word of thieves.'

The word triggered the connection in their minds at the same time. The Winters looked at each other with the sudden realization about the probable identity of the men. The news reported three escaped criminals traveling through the outback with the police warning, do not approach and are *considered armed and dangerous*. Dane's eyes warned his brother and sister to say nothing, but they saw him tighten his reins, and they did the same, ready to follow him the instant he gave the signal to ride off.

'Now, that ain't nice, is it, boy?' Jake's voice was threateningly low, and he took a step towards them. 'Maybe we should just keep you here until your parents arrive, and they can make you apologize.'

With an imperceptible movement of his hand, Dane asked Misty to back a few steps. Lani and Matthew did the same. To the casual observer, it looked like the horses had decided to back up on their own and were simply nervous. Dane continued to glare at the men, hiding his unease about what might happen if they held guns behind their backs. They could only be handguns, the thought to himself, not rifles, and if we can get away quick enough, their aim with handguns on moving targets is not likely to be accurate. Could he risk that chance?

Jake looked at them closely. He had not missed the glance they shared when they realized who the 'thieves' were, and that changed the situation. If they had known who they were before they rode up, they would not have approached, but he could see by their sudden wariness that they knew now. He also judged that the oldest boy was considering making a run for it, and he did not want that happening until he had thought the situation through. How quickly could the parents contact the police? How could they make a clean escape from this? How could they buy some time? If he held the kids until the parents arrived, then maybe they could tie them all up and call someone in a day or two to make sure they didn't die here. Or they could kill them all, hide the bodies, and have even more time.

Taking the gun from behind his back, Jake pointed it at Dane, Lani, and Matthew, the barrel moving from one to another. Skinner produced his weapon as well and held it loosely in front of him. Jake had to give them credit; they did not flinch but sat there on their horses looking directly at him, their eyes intense as their minds raced at a million clicks a minute assessing everything. He nodded to himself. There was no doubt that outback kids had it all over their city counterparts – these kids weren't fazed at all; they were trying to figure a way out.

'You know what this is?' he asked them.

'357 magnum revolver,' Matthew replied stiffly. Their father had owned one - a licensed firearm which was sold to a gun dealer after he died.

Jake was not surprised by his knowledge. He remembered that kids out here knew their guns. 'Then you know what it can do to you. So get off your horses and come over here, and we'll wait for your parents together, OK?'

Dane shook his head. 'You just get going,' he said without as much as a tremor in his voice to betray the fear he held for his brother and sister. 'Take the ute and drive out of here.'

'And get how far?' Jake sniffed and shook his head. 'That just isn't going to work for us 'cause I figure you're going to call the cops as soon as we're out of sight, so we have a new plan.'

Once more, the reins tightened, and Jake sensed that the riders were about to make a run for it, which would be a shame because then he'd have to kill them all, and he was a crack shot, he wouldn't miss. He saw them glance at one another.

'Don't try it,' he warned them, 'you won't make it. Get off your horses.'

They still sat there, and he knew it was time to teach them a lesson. He looked from one to the other: the youngest, the girl, the eldest; the gun moving from face to face. It moved back to Lani; he dipped the barrel and pulled the trigger.

CHAPTER TEN
Amy and Brandon
2.45 pm – 3.40 pm

'They better appreciate us bringing this fruit back for them,' Brandon grumbled without ire as they walked along on a loose rein. 'I think I have mango juice dripping down my jeans. I should have picked them green mangoes.'

'Some of my bananas are a bit squished,' Amy admitted with a chuckle, 'but that's where banana smoothies come in - in the blender with some ice cream, and they'll taste great.'

'Do you reckon we'll see any Min Min lights tonight?' Brandon changed the subject.

'Probably not. If they're only seen a few times a year, it's not all that likely that we're going to see them just because we're here looking for them.'

'Yeah, I guess,' Brandon nodded and thought about the camping trip in general. 'Even if we don't see them, it's a good way to spend a few days.'

Amy took the time to look around at the clear sky that climbed from faded shades at the horizon to deep blue overhead, the ochre reds of the hills with their purple shadows, the trees, and the stretching plains of grasses. In front of her horse, Blaze trotted along, sniffing the ground for all the scents that told him stories of what had passed this way. She breathed in the hot, dry air and closed her eyes, savoring the outback as she felt the swaying walk of her horse beneath her. It sure was a good way to spend a few days.

'It's great,' she agreed. 'We should do it every year, forever. I don't want to grow so old and serious that I couldn't enjoy doing something like this with friends.'

'We probably will, though,' he shrugged, 'we'll all grow apart and go on with our own lives. It's just what happens.'

Amy shook her head, 'Nup, I'm not going to let it. I want us all to stay friends all through life. I have a plan.'

Grinning at her, Brandon put on a funny voice, 'Ah, a cunning plan! What is this cunning plan?'

Rolling her eyes at his comedy act, Amy explained, 'It's just what I've said before about us all becoming great riders. The horse world is such a small world that if we all go on riding and competing, it doesn't matter what we compete in, we'll still be friends and still be seeing each other and helping each other.'

'The outback riders who take on the world?'

She met his eyes and dazzled him with a smile lit by a thousand dreams. 'The outback riders who conquer the world,' she amended. 'We're all born to ride, every one of us. Do you realize how far ahead that puts us when we ride as though we are part of our horses? Some riders take years and years of training to ride how well you do, and they still don't get it, and it just comes naturally to you and me and my cousins. We have the ability, and if we can all share the dream, all we need is the courage to fly. And we will. We will soar. I know we will.'

For a moment, he held her gaze and felt inspired. She

was right. They could achieve whatever they wished if they worked hard enough and aimed high enough.

'So, you think Nu-man and I could make it in cutting?'

'If you plan it out properly,' she nodded, 'Dad always used to tell me that in a journey a lifetime long, step one was having the dream, step two was making plans, and then you had a million steps of hard work. I don't know much about cutting, but I planned to learn as much as I could about eventing from books, videos, and clinics. I watch the best in the world, and I'll go to their trainers. I go to clinics, train, compete, and improve, and train some more.'

'Sounds dedicated,' he looked at her closely. 'Don't you ever just want to slack off and be a teenager?'

'I did before Dad died. He'd told me that life was too brief to fill it with nothing, like just sitting around watching TV. He said we needed to dream, and believe, and achieve. He didn't care if my dreams were about being the best hairdresser in the world, growing the best vegetables, or being the best three-day event rider. Dreams, he said, were like the colors of our lives, and I should use them to paint a beautiful picture of my life and not die after living a colorless life of nothing. And then he died. I didn't waste much time after that. I mean, I still play X-box and watch TV, but that's not living; that's just passing the time.'

'And then Mr. Winter died, too,' Brandon shook his head sadly at that. Geoff Winter had always treated him kindly and welcomed him into the Winter household.

'Life's too short for some people,' Amy sighed, thinking of her Uncle Geoff. 'I wish they didn't have to die.'

They fell into silence and rode their horses down into the creek bed, following it as it wound its way towards their campsite, the horses' hooves soft on the sand. Amy asked about Brandon's station, and he fell into describing his life there, skipping over the parts about his parents' drinking and telling her about the history of the property and his animals. They were still talking about this when they rode up out of the creek. They topped the bank and saw the extra car parked at the campsite about fifty meters away.

'Who's that?' Amy turned to Brandon, a questioning look on her face.

He shook his head, 'No idea, I don't know the car, but they're talking to the others.'

They could see the backs of two men and the hand of a third on the other side of the gooseneck while Dane, Lani, and Matthew sat on their horses facing them. The Winters were at a slight angle to Amy and Brandon, so they didn't notice the two riders coming out of the creek. Something about the tenseness of the scene disturbed Amy and Brandon. They halted, trying to work out what was going on, while Blaze whined softly at their side. Then Amy saw one of the men move his hands to the left and right and caught a glimpse of a gun pointing at her cousins.

The gun jerked, and Fleet crumpled to the ground. A split second later, the sound reached them, but the image of Fleet dying was too horrifying for Amy to even think about the sound of the gunfire. Fleet's legs had just given away like a puppet whose strings were released, and he sat on the ground with his head folded under as though he was praying. She could see the tragic shock on Lani's face as she sat in the saddle with her horse dead beneath her.

Brandon let out a string of swear words, then he hissed at her, 'Get back!' He slapped her lightly on the arm to knock her out of her frozen state and motioned towards the creek.

He spun Nu-man around and scrambled back down the creek bank with Amy right on his heels, calling for Blaze to follow. With the bank several meters above their heads, the people at the campsite could not see them. With the shrubs, trees, and winding sandbanks to absorb the noise, their voices were unlikely to carry to those at the gooseneck.

Amy stared at Brandon, her eyes wide with fear and questions, her heart galloping from the massive rush of adrenalin coursing through her system, her skin pale and clammy from the shock. A dozen possible actions raced through her mind, dismissed as quickly as they appeared. Aunt Eleanor: away at March's for the rest of the day and night, and Amy wouldn't want her aunt to face three men with guns. Uncle John: away at Winton until tomorrow. The Winfields at Marantha station: the radio to call them was in the truck; there was no mobile phone reception here, so they didn't even carry mobile phones; Marantha was over twenty-five kilometers away.

The closest stations, apart from Sunhaven and Uncle John's Brindella Fells, had been bought up by overseas companies, and no one lived in the homesteads, so there was no help there. They could ride to the campsite and risk having the criminals shoot them. That would not help anyone - they had to remain undetected. They had to work out how to do something themselves.

'There's no one who can help us,' Brandon whispered, and Amy knew all the thoughts that raced through her mind had also gone through his. 'Mrs. Winter and John aren't home, and we can't contact Marantha Station.'

Amy rubbed her hands over her eyes, trying to think. She patted Days, who was restless from the nervousness he was picking up from her, and spoke softly, 'We'll come up with something. We have to.'

'They'll be the escaped prisoners we heard about,' Brandon began, then stopped, shaking his head, thinking of the huge odds against the criminals being here in an area as big as the outback. 'I don't know what we can do, but we'll do something.'

'You don't suppose they'll just get in their car and go?'

Brandon shook his head doubtfully, trying to think of all the clues he'd seen in the few seconds that they'd been looking at the drama being played out at the campsite. He tried to piece them together. 'Their car looked empty, and Gertie was loaded up, so I think they mean to take her. They wouldn't swap any car for Gertie unless their car broke down. It also means they've probably already started her to see that she goes. That means she won't want to start for the rest of the day unless they know her little tricks – and they won't. So now they won't be going anywhere unless they take your truck or don't touch Gertie for three or four hours, which is unlikely.'

'I wish they'd just take the truck and leave right now,' Amy shut her eyes trying to concentrate, 'but they may as well hang a big neon sign over their head with an arrow pointing to them.'

'Yeah, it's way too easy to spot from the air. Little Gertie would fit right in with all the other old four-wheel-drives on the road until they swap her for something else.'

Amy felt a wave of nausea sweep over her as she thought of Lani's stricken face when Fleet was killed underneath her. Lani would be devastated - she loved that horse so much. Instead of being able to grieve for him, she was facing three men who could easily kill the other horses or their riders. They had to do something.

'Do you think they'll kill them?' she asked, her voice still hushed so that there was no chance of the sound carrying to the men.

Taking a deep breath to calm his nerves and leaning over the front of Nu-man's saddle as though in pain, Brandon thought about this. Finally, he shook his head. 'I think if they were going to kill them, they'd have done it already. They shot Fleet as a warning. I wonder if they know we're out here somewhere.'

'They'll have to know that there are more than just Dane, Lani, and Matty,' Amy pointed out, 'there are three slept-in beds in the back of the gooseneck and ours in the front, so they're going to figure there's more than three of us.'

'They won't have told them about us,' Brandon spoke slowly, trying to think through everything from Dane's point of view, wondering what he would do in the same position. 'They wouldn't want them thinking they're only up against a bunch of kids. Dane will have said that their father or their parents are out here.'

'Which would have been a good bluff if they were just stealing a bit of stuff,' said Amy softly, following on with his train of thought, 'but the news said those men are killers. I think they'll wait for the rest of the family – that's us - to come back before doing anything. They'll use Dane, Lani, and Matty as hostages if they need to…they'll want to do whatever it takes to give them the biggest head start on police.'

'So they could mean to get us all together and kill us all,' Brandon ignored Amy's sudden intake of breath at that idea. They had to consider it. 'Then they'll have to hope no one comes looking for us for a few days. Or maybe they'll leave us all tied up so that we can tell the police who did it when someone finds us. Perhaps they'll take a hostage or two to keep the others silent.'

Amy nodded, following his line of thinking. 'They can't take us all with them as we can't all fit in the back of Gertie.'

'And I don't think they'll want any more murders hanging over their heads because that makes sure everyone, everywhere, is looking for them even harder. I think they'll avoid that if they can.' His voice sounded less hopeful than his words.

'Maybe,' Amy was not convinced, 'or perhaps they don't care whether they kill again or not. Whatever - we have to do something. We can't just wait it out here in the creek and hope they leave. How long would it take to ride to Marantha?'

'Too long - an hour and a bit at horse-killing pace in this heat. You'd be better riding back to Sunhaven and calling for help from there.'

'Both of us?'

Brandon thought for a few seconds, his mind weighing up all the possible courses of action and likely outcomes. 'You go,' he told her, 'it'll take you and Days about forty minutes at a good cross country pace - don't overheat him. I'll stay here and keep an eye on things. Not that there's anything I can do, but Nu-man wouldn't handle a hard ride like that. Call everyone – the police, the fire, the rescue services, Mrs. Winter, the neighbors, everyone.'

'Don't do anything while I'm gone,' Amy warned him, worried he would try some hero act that would end up with him or her cousins injured. 'Just wait here and don't be a hero.'

'Don't worry,' he assured her with a lop-sided smile. 'When it comes to looking down the barrel of a gun, I'm the world's biggest coward. I won't be going near them.'

As though to prove he had no intention of riding into battle against the escapees, Brandon dismounted and took the reins over Nu-man's head. 'I'll wait here until you get back, or I might go a bit further up the creek so I'm not as close. Look for me in the creek when you get back.'

Amy gathered up her reins and tried to think if there was anything else she needed to know before going. She knew how to get home by following the creek for a few kilometers and, once out of sight of the camp, coming up and following the road back to Sunhaven. She knew who to call and she knew how to describe the location of the campsite.

'I think I have it covered,' she told him, looking down into his eyes as he stood next to his horse.

He was worried about her heading off by herself but didn't want to say anything in case she took it to mean that he had doubts about her ability to do the task. That didn't worry him. It concerned him that the men might see her, or Days might stumble and fall while she was alone out there. He felt that they should stay together, but he knew only Days was suitable for the ride back to Sunhaven as young Nu-man would knock up long before he made it there. Nu-man was built for stopping and turning, not galloping long distances in punishing heat. Brandon could not suppress the overriding urge to protect her, and sending her out into the paddock to ride back to Sunhaven alone went against that instinct.

As though reading his mind, she said, 'I'll be fine - I know my way home, and I'll leave Days there and bring Laddie back. You should see some of the cross country courses I've ridden!'

He grinned at her, winked, and gave her leg a quick pat, 'I know, you're the girl who jumped over Legend's Leap; you can handle anything.'

Blushing at his words and that roguish wink, Amy mumbled a few words about it becoming a habit of riding for help when the Winters were in trouble. Then she turned Days away and pushed him up into a canter along the sandy floor of the creek bed, heading away from the hills with Blaze running close behind. She leaned forward in a jumping position to give his hindquarters unhindered movement and guided him around the roughest sections of the ground. Choosing a good half pace that matched the rough terrain and would leave him enough wind to make the full distance, Amy concentrated on watching the path ahead, looking for any obstacles or holes that could cause problems for her horse.

Once in cross country mode, she managed to push the fears about her cousins out of her mind and exist in a world where only her horse, the path ahead, and the ultimate destination mattered. The heat stopped affecting her. The death of Fleet moved out her thoughts. Her world was just the ground, the points where Days' hooves were landing, and the rhythm of his nodding head and flashing legs.

There had been many times when she had galloped Days over rough ground, so she knew how to handle the pace, and they quickly settled into stride. They had gone several hundred meters when they passed alongside a long, narrow waterhole, and neither horse nor rider noticed the half a dozen feral pigs lying motionless in the mud at the edge of the water, their black coats camouflaged in the dark mud. As Days came within ten meters of them, they erupted out of the water with grunts and squeals that were terrifying to a horse. The smell of the pigs hit his nostrils in the same instant that he saw the creatures explode from the mud.

In mid-stride, he changed direction, throwing his body to the side away from the feral pigs. Despite the sudden swerve, Amy stuck to him as though welded to the saddle, and she quickly sat up to get her weight behind his movement. In that position, she could go with him if he changed direction again or stopped and not end up being catapulted out of the saddle and over his shoulders. In a desperate second, she tried to watch the ground as she put the brakes on Days and also kept an eye out for the pigs, which were running in all directions.

One of the largest, his face covered with wet, black mud so that his long tusks looked alarmingly white against it, rushed straight for the creek bank and went under Days' legs. The palomino lurched as he tried to jump it, but his forelegs caught either side of the rock-hard creature, and he began to somersault. Amy felt the fall coming and knew there was nothing she could do to stop it. She dropped her reins to free up Days' head as he began the revolution through the air. Then she kicked her feet free from the stirrups as this was not something she wanted to ride to the ground. She had seen a rider killed in a fall when the horse somersaulted and landed on him. Getting out from under the falling body of the horse was paramount.

As the front of Days' face drove into the sand, forcing a mighty grunt out of him, his body began cart-wheeling over so that his hindquarters were straight up in the air. Amy looked to the side and pushed herself out of the saddle, aiming to land in the sand away from where Days was going to fall. It all played out slowly in her mind and, though she wished she could help her horse, she knew she had to let him fall and hope that he would survive without any broken bones or pulled muscles.

Hitting the sand crookedly, Amy felt the breath get smashed out of her, and she rolled out of the way as her horse came crashing down. He hit heavily, spine first, all four legs in the air, then he tumbled to one side and lay still. Amy tried to move to help him, but she felt paralyzed, unable to breathe, and an instant of panic overtook her as she realized she had broken her back, and her lungs could not work. She would be dead in minutes. Blaze whimpered at her side, pressing his nose against her and pawing at her in worry. Panic rose madly within her as she struggled to breathe but could not get air in or out of her lungs.

In the space of a few seconds, she knew she was

winded, not paralyzed. Her lungs were refusing to work, which had tricked her mind into thinking she had broken her back. Forcing herself to stay calm, she lay until her stunned diaphragm began working again, and she could gasp in the hot, dry air with shuddering gulps. Rolling over to her hands and knees, she gave the faithful kelpie a quick pat then crawled over to where Days lay in the sand, his sides heaving so she knew he was alive. Before she reached him, he struggled to his feet and stood there with his head low, shaking, looking at her apologetically.

They had suffered their share of spills over jumps before, and he knew to wait until Amy caught him. Before she could stand and take his reins, several piglets ran in front of him, squealing loudly for their mother, who came snuffling back down the creek bank at him. Amy grabbed at Blaze to make sure he did not chase the piglets, but their noise was too much for Days. He let out a loud snort, threw his head up, and spun away from the pigs, taking off at a gallop back to Brandon and Nu-man.

'At least you're not lame,' she muttered after him, his white tail pluming out behind him as he disappeared around a bend in the creek, showing no sign of stopping until he reached the other horse. Standing and dusting herself off, she grimaced at the piglets that ran after their mother. 'Obviously, my horse does not like you pigs.'

The big sow gathered up her piglets and trotted off, only stopping once to turn and glare at Amy, but she was not too worried. She had one eye on a nearby tree in case she needed to climb to safety away from the ripping tusks of the razorback. She had learned enough about feral pigs to know that they were very dangerous if they were injured or if they had been chased and were hot, but cool rested pigs like these tended to run when faced with people. These were running.

Breaking into a loose-limbed jog, she followed the hoof prints back up the creek towards Brandon and his horse.

Brandon was leading Nu-man to a spot further from the camp when he heard the muffled sounds of a galloping horse coming back up the creek. He turned to see Days charging at them, flat gallop, a look of fear on his face. His heart did a painful tattoo in his chest when he realized that Amy was not in the saddle, and there was damp sand on the palomino's face showing that he had taken a fall. As Days neared him, he began to slow, and Brandon readied himself to grab at the trailing reins and catch the frightened horse.

Nu-man moved nervously as the bigger horse bore down on them. Brandon turned to calm him down, hoping he would keep his horse settled as he caught Amy's horse. When Days was less than twenty meters away and had slowed to a canter, Nu-man was still running backward, his eyes startled at the sight of Days coming at them. He began dragging Brandon with him as he tried to escape what he perceived as an attack from the older horse.

'Steady, boy,' Brandon crooned to him, staying calm so that Nu-man could draw courage from him, 'it's just that big yella horse, and I'm going to catch him, so you stay calm.'

A mob of twenty grey kangaroos bounded down the creek, almost running into Days before bouncing in all directions. That was too much for Days to handle. Already stressed from the pigs and falling, he accelerated back into a full gallop towards Brandon and the younger gelding. Nu-man flung himself around, ignoring Brandon gripping the reins, and took off along the creek bed towards the hills, forcing Brandon to release him or risk being dragged.

Sparing a few seconds to watch the two galloping horses vanish around the next bend, Brandon shook his head, sighed, and angrily kicked at the sand. He blamed himself for not keeping his horse calm – the horses were just being horses, and he should have handled things better. Turning, he ran down the creek to where he hoped to find Amy with nothing more serious than a light dusting of sand from a tumble. If she was injured, or worse… he did not want to even think about the possibility and ran harder to try and block out any of those thoughts.

When he rounded an outcropping of rock in the creek and saw Amy jogging towards him, the brown dog at her side, looking none the worse for having lost her horse, he stopped. Leaning over, his hands resting on his knees, he drew in huge breaths to try and get his wind back. He had not realized how much energy he had put into running to find Amy until he halted, and then the screaming complaints from his oxygen-deprived leg muscles made themselves heard. It was not something he wanted to think about at the moment and certainly not something he even understood, but when he caught sight of Amy, he felt an enormous rush of relief that made him light-headed.

'I'm sorry,' Amy looked at him miserably as she approached, her large green eyes welling with tears. She felt responsible for ruining their chance of getting help for her cousins. 'Days fell. There were pigs. I couldn't catch him…'

Brandon acted without thinking. He stepped forward and wrapped his arms around her, holding her close. It seemed right to comfort her and hold her in the safety of his arms. She was not like the girls he flirted with at pony club or school, the ones he might try to cuddle and kiss because it was fun. This was different. He wanted to keep her safe, and when he saw the misery in her eyes, he felt the need to protect her.

'I'm sorry, too,' he whispered against her hair. 'I tried to hold Nu-man, but he had a panic attack and got away from me. Both of them took off up the creek. We can hope that they pull up somewhere so we can catch them.'

Amy closed her eyes and spent several seconds enjoying the sensations of being held by Brandon. She had never let any boy hold her like that before. She had never wanted any boy to hold her so closely. Now she did not want him to let her go.

Raised voices from the campsite interrupted their moment, and they broke apart, looking at each other silently with trepidation. What was happening up there?

They crawled up the creek bank until they could see over the edge without being easy to spot from the camp. Amy kept a hand on Blaze to make sure he stayed with her and did not start barking. In the camp, Lani was catching Nu-man and Days while the men waved their guns around. It appeared that the two runaways had followed the creek up towards the hills, and when the banks were not as high so that they could see out of the creek bed to the campsite, they had headed there to the company of the other horses. Dane and Matthew stood with their horses, remaining as still as possible as one of the men kept swinging his gun towards them in a clear message about not moving. Amy held her breath, hoping they would not shoot her horse, but it seemed that killing Fleet had been enough bloodletting for now, and they were directing Lani to hold the new arrivals.

The three men seemed intent on watching the Winters and were showing no signs of turning around. Brandon gave Amy's arm a quick tug as he stood up. She understood what he wanted and rose to her feet beside him. If any of her cousins saw them, they would know that they were OK and watching the camp but unable to go for help because of losing their horses. For several seconds they stood, risking being seen by the men if they turned around, but Amy knew it was important for her cousins to know they were uninjured and nearby. No one appeared to notice them. Dane moved his left hand carelessly as though wiping something from his eye, and both Brandon and Amy caught the meaning as his index finger pointed at his chest before touching his eye and curling towards them as he looked down at his feet. *I see you.*

Brandon slipped down the bank to sit with his back to it, his boots pushing out mounds of sand, and his shoulders slumped. 'Well, they know we're here and that we don't have our horses, so they know we're not going to get the police any time soon.'

Sitting beside him, Blaze in her lap, Amy took a deep breath and tried to think of what they could do, 'We'll come up with something.'

When Brandon looked at her skeptically, she met his gaze and tried to find the words to explain how she saw him and her cousins. They were so capable; they drove cars and trucks; they faced floods and fires. The most dangerous snakes in the world did not worry them. They could use rifles and shotguns and handle whatever life threw at them with the ease of people who knew they would cope. They were happy in the city at school surrounded by people, and content in the middle of the outback without seeing anyone else for weeks on end. If the end of the world came, these were the people she would want beside her because they would find a way to survive.

She smiled at him, 'You outback guys know more about everything than any people I've ever met. You'll think of something. We'll work this out. I absolutely believe it will work out, and you'll learn that I'm never wrong about these feelings.'

'Psychic?' he asked her, his eyebrows raised half questioningly, half teasingly.

'I'm hoping so.'

'OK,' he squared his shoulders back, 'let's figure out what we can do.'

CHAPTER ELEVEN
Dane, Lani, and Matthew
3.10 pm – 4 pm

Lani froze as the gun swayed between her brothers and herself, one hand holding Fleet's reins firm while the other stroked his shoulder near his wither to keep him calm as he sensed her fear. He was attuned to her emotions, as is the way with most horses and their riders, and if she worried about something, he would become nervous. She did not want to be on a restless horse with a man pointing a gun at them.

They were familiar with guns, but they had never looked down the barrel of one before as it had been drilled into them to never point a gun at anyone. Their father's repeated phrase, *it's the unloaded gun that kills someone,* reminded them how dangerous they were and how easily a person could be shot by accident if the handler assumed it was unloaded. One of the few times she'd ever seen her father so angry that he raised his voice at them was when Dane had pointed a realistic-looking toy gun at Matthew while playing. So to be looking at the black hole of a gun directed at them chilled her to the core, and she knew her brothers would feel the same.

They did not panic. The Winters had grown up in a harsh land where danger was never far away. Their bodies just went still and non-threatening as their brains raced frantically to deal with the situation.

When the gun settled on Lani and the barrel dropped slightly, her heart stopped. She knew what he was about to do in that second before he pulled the trigger, and a wave of terror swept over her. Not Fleet! Not her horse. Her dearest friend in times of trouble, her courage, her heart. The gun exploded, and Fleet dropped from underneath her as though the earth had given way.

There was no struggle, no sound from him apart from the deadened thud of his body hitting the ground - a noise not unlike meat dropped on a bench. He was there one moment, full of life and linked to her spirit in that indefinable way that horses and their people know each other, and then he was gone, the link broken. The energy that flowed between them whenever they were together was severed, and the remains hung from her heart like a torn ribbon no longer connected to him. He was gone.

With her feet still in the stirrups that rested on the ground on either side of Fleet's body, she flung herself over his neck for the final hug, and her heart shattered over the loss of her friend. Matthew and Dane looked down at her, a reflected agony in their eyes. He had been with them for so many shows, so many polocrosse carnivals and musters. He was family. They wanted to comfort their sister, but there were still two guns pointing at them, and they knew that their survival might depend on them being calm and quiet.

'If you don't want your other horses to join him,' Jake spoke without any emotion as he regarded the girl crying over her dead horse - it meant nothing to him, 'you'd better do as you're told. Make a run for it, and the horses die before you do, and maybe I won't kill them so quick next time.'

'We're not running,' Dane spoke in a clear voice that sounded calmer than he felt. When dealing with dangerous and unpredictable animals, he was taught to watch them closely, appear calm but not aggressive, and keep movements to a minimum. Sudden actions like waving hands and quickly turning heads could aggravate touchy animals like the three standing in front of him. *Keep as still as possible,* he repeated to himself. He knew Matthew would have the same response and, once Lani began to think after her initial shock of losing Fleet, she would be the same. 'Tell us what you want us to do, and we'll do what we can to get you out of here and on your way to wherever you're going.'

'When will your parents get back here?' Jake barked at him.

Dane considered telling the truth but realized they were not likely to believe that five children were camping alone in the middle of nowhere, and perhaps thinking that two adults were out there somewhere might provide some insurance. He had glimpsed Brandon and Amy heading back down into the creek after the gun had been fired and knew they would be working on getting help. He looked at Matthew and, from the very quick motion of his brother's eyes at the creek and back, knew he had seen them, too.

We'll be OK, he said silently with his eyes to Matthew.

I know, the silent look came back at him.

'They won't be back for a while,' Dane replied, trying to find a vague answer that he could change if required. 'They've ridden into the hills.'

'That gunshot will bring them back,' Meat nodded

knowingly as he helped himself to another of Eleanor's biscuits.

'They might not have heard it,' Dane pointed out carefully, trying to come up with a scenario that would explain the prolonged absence of their invented parents. They needed to give Brandon and Amy time to get help. 'If they did, they'd probably think it was just the jackaroos from down the road shooting something. They were near here earlier today shooting pigs.'

Jake seemed to accept that. 'Get off your horses, then, and we'll wait a bit as we think what we're gunna do.'

Looking down at Lani, who was now kneeling in the dust by Fleet's head, crying softly into his mane as she stroked his face, Dane asked, 'Can I help my sister?'

'Don't worry me,' Jake shrugged. 'Just don't think of doing anything stupid, or you'll have more horses to cry over.'

'Just shoot 'em now,' Meat said with sadistic enthusiasm – he enjoyed watching things die.

'I will if these kids don't do the right thing,' Jake scowled at them.

With an almost imperceptible nod at his brother to tell him to dismount, they both stepped off their horses. Dane handed his reins to Matthew, who stood bravely, chin up, trying not to think of how he would feel if it was Shandy lying there dead. Dane walked to Lani and knelt beside her, one arm over her shoulders as he used his other hand to arrange Fleet's long forelock over the hole in the middle of his forehead that ran with blood.

'Cry for him later,' he whispered to her, squeezing her shoulders slightly to make her listen to his softly spoken words that were for her ears only. 'I need you to help us. Brandon and Amy were in the creek just behind the gooseneck, and they'll be going for help now. We need to get through this.'

Lani turned her tear-stained face towards him, and he felt the raw agony of her loss when he met her eyes and his own filled with tears. 'I know,' he whispered, 'I know, Lani, but we need you now. We'll all mourn Fleet tomorrow, OK?'

She nodded. Her hands slowly moved away from her horse, and for a moment, she stared at the pool of blood that was spreading across the ground under his head — the bright red arterial blood mixed with the oxygen-exhausted dark, almost black blood from the veins. Fleet's life force had been in that blood, and now it was... she looked to the sky... it was where? She wondered. Where had he gone? This body was just the house where Fleet had lived, and his spirit, his soul, had been so much more than this dead mass. Where had Fleet's energy gone?

Another look into her brother's eyes told her that he understood what she was feeling, and she understood the gravity of his words. They needed to survive. Tomorrow, they would say goodbye to Fleet. With a huge effort, she put aside her thoughts about her horse and focussed on the task at hand: staying alive.

They joined Matthew and waited while the three men discussed their plans. From what the Winters could hear, they were torn between several possibilities. They could tie the children up and leave now, hoping that the 'parents' would not be back for several hours, and if they disabled the truck, it would be several more hours before they would be able to raise the alarm. They could wait for the parents and tie them all up, then leave, and that might give them a head start of a day or two. The heaviest built man seemed to favor waiting until the parents returned and killing them all so that no one was left to tell the police who had committed the crime. If they did that, they might get away altogether without anyone knowing they were the ones who had passed this way.

'It'll take a bit over half an hour for Amy and Days to get home,' Dane spoke softly, trying to move his lips as little as possible so that their conversation might pass unnoticed by the men, 'and a fair bit longer than that for the police to get here as they'll probably drive, not fly.'

He paused and checked that his brother and sister were following along and not disagreeing on any point. Satisfied that they were with him so far, he continued, 'We're going to have to be ready for whatever comes about in the next few hours. Matthew, if you get the chance to get away, no matter what else is going on, you get on Shandy and ride like hell out of here. OK?'

'I'm not leaving you,' he said through the side of his mouth.

'You'll go,' Lani said firmly, 'if you get the chance, you *will* go, Matthew, you understand?'

'Brandon will be in that creek somewhere,' Dane guessed, 'he'll send Amy back home because Days will be fine with a long run like that, so you'll go and find him if you get the chance. You'll be more help to us out there with Brandon than stuck here with us.'

'They'll shoot Misty,' Matthew looked at his brother's horse.

'Matty, as great as Misty is, I can always get another horse - I can't get another little brother. Promise me you'll run if you get the chance.'

Matthew shrugged, a reluctant agreement to the request.

'And you'll take Misty and go if you have the chance,' Dane instructed Lani. 'If we get any sort of distraction, you get out of here, too.'

Lani gave him a rebellious look and agreed, but only to hold Matthew to his promise. She had no intention of leaving her older brother - she would not leave unless they rode out together on Misty.

'And no matter what, don't make them angry,' Dane continued. 'We don't want to give them any excuse to think killing us would be a good idea.'

'They're going to get pretty angry if I ride away and fairly angsty when our parents don't turn up,' pointed out Matthew.

'We'll handle that – if you get the chance, you have to run. As for our parents…we'll tell them that they found the gold they've been looking for, and they'll believe us because we'll say it like we believe it.'

'Gold? Around here?' Lani gave him an incredulous look. 'Let's hope they get in Gertie and just leave.'

The men turned their attention back to the three Winters. Jake stepped forward, waving his gun at them, indicating that he wanted them to move apart from each other. When they had a couple of steps between them, he ordered them to listen carefully.

'You're going to tie those horses up,' he told them, as he squatted down on his heels and carelessly waved the flies away from his face with the gun. 'Then we're going to tie you up and get out of here. Meat over there, he wants to kill you, but I've never been much for violence against kids because I know what happens to blokes who do that sort of stuff when they get to the big house. You'd better understand that it'd be good for youse if you weren't too clear about who was here or how many of us you saw because the bigger the start we get on the cops, the further we're going to get and the less likely that we'll get caught.'

He paused to point the gun at each one of them in turn, 'We get caught, and I'm gunna blame you lot, and even if we're back inside, I'll send someone here to kill your horses and maybe your parents. Got me?'

The three Winters nodded and looked suitably frightened, which they were, but not frightened senseless, which is what Jake assumed. Their minds were working rapidly, looking for ideas and options and trying to think of all possibilities and outcomes

'Good,' he nodded, 'I thought youse all looked smart, so it seems we're on the same page here. We get away safe, and your family and your horses stay safe. My other buddy has already killed your two-way in the truck, and your phones are in a bucket of water, so don't think you'll call anyone, right?'

They nodded without pointing out that the phones had no reception here, anyway, so they were not so much mobile phones as they were mobile devices for games, music, photos, and videos.

'And Meat here, he wants to do something more permanent than leaving you tied up, so don't get him riled up, or maybe I won't be able to stop him. Got me?'

Meat scrounged through one of the bags they'd transferred from their car to Gertie and pulled out a pack of plastic zip ties. Dane knew how strong they were - once their wrists and ankles were bound, their chance of escaping or fighting back would decrease drastically. Then, once the men discovered that Gertie would not start twice in the one day without the tricks Brandon knew, they might think of taking them along in the gooseneck or even killing them. Dane was fully aware of the killing lust in Meat's eyes every time he looked at them. He had to come up with something that would keep them unbound.

A voice seemed to speak inside Dane's head. It was a memory of his father telling him how to handle bad-natured horses. 'Sometimes, you can't fight them head-on. They're bigger and stronger than you, and you don't want to let them know that,' Geoff Winter had told him once when they were handling some five-year-old Thoroughbreds from one of the neighboring properties. They were big, strong horses that had never been taught to lead or handled in any way apart from being roped and branded as yearlings, so they did not have any good memories of people. 'So, don't try and fight them at their own game with strength - distract them. Don't confront them - side-track them. Make them move to your song - don't jump around to theirs. Use your brain to out-think them.'

Dane drew a deep breath as the vague form of a plan began to take shape in his mind. He glanced at his brother and sister quickly, and they read the *play along with me* message in his eyes and, even though they did not move, he saw the agreement in theirs.

'I think you'll have lots of time to make your getaway. Mum and Dad might not get back until well after dark if they find what they've been looking for.'

'Don't say anything!' Lani hissed at him, throwing an alarmed look at the men.

It worked – they were interested.

'Yeah, shut up, Dane!' Matthew gave him an angry look.

Meat had been approaching them with the zip ties, but their words made him stop and look from one to the other. 'And what are they looking for?' he asked with an amused look on his face. 'Bone hunters, are they? Looking for dinosaur bones? Maybe looking for a needle in a haystack,' he guffawed at his nonsense.

'May as well be,' Dane grumbled looking at the ground, a sour expression on his face. 'They've spent four years looking for it, and they said they found it this time, but it's hard to believe it's real.'

'Don't say any more,' pleaded Lani, not sure what Dane was playing at but following his lead convincingly. 'What if they have found it? Just shut up and let the men tie us up and get on their way.'

'Found what?' Skinner asked, the curiosity in his dull mind finally roused.

'Forget it,' Dane said, holding his wrists out to Meat, 'tie us up and keep going. You'll get a big head start because they probably won't get back till after dark.'

Skinner stepped in closer to Dane and snarled at him, 'Found what, kid? What are they looking for?'

'It's probably not even real,' Dane hesitated as though resisting telling them the truth about his parents' whereabouts. 'People have looked for it for over a hundred years. I don't think it exists. Honest - it's just a dream.'

'Lost treasure?' asked Skinner hopefully, his eyes lighting up.

'Not exactly,' Dane shook his head, 'but I can tell you this – you're likely to get away without any of us saying anything because if they have found it, they won't be telling anyone about you being here because they won't want the police or anyone else to know what they've found. Having our car stolen and being tied up will be nothing compared to finding…' he stumbled over his words as though he had been about to name something, 'finding it.'

Jake had had enough of riddles. He raised his gun and said, 'Which horse do I have to shoot first before you spit it out, boy? What are they looking for?'

Looking at his brother and sister, who gave him suitably angry looks, Dane shook his head as though upset about being forced to reveal the secret. 'Lasseter's Reef,' he announced, 'it was always thought to be over towards Western Australia from here, but they reversed his directions, did some other calculations, and came up with the Sunhaven Hills. They say it's in these hills.'

The name 'Lasseter's Reef' meant nothing to Skinner

and Meat, who stared blankly at Dane, wondering what a reef was doing so far from the ocean, but Jake knew something of the story and took the bait. His eyes gleamed with the start of the sickness that had kept Lasseter searching for his lost reef for thirty years after first finding it, the same sickness that had seen hundreds trek through the remotest parts of Australia desperate to find Lasseter's Reef. Gold fever.

'Once you have the horse's attention,' the memory of his father's voice continued inside his head, 'then you are in control. You can't do anything with him while he's not listening or while he thinks he can push you around, but once you have his ears, eyes, and mind on you, you are the boss. Hold his attention and stay in charge.'

'No one's ever found gold in these parts,' guessed Jake; he was not sure, but he thought opals were more likely to be found in central-western Queensland than gold.

'No one except Lasseter,' Dane glanced at the hills, his mind racing madly behind his composed expression, trying to piece together a convincing story that might lead somewhere. 'Dad said the hills are the remains of a volcanic eruption from hundreds of millions of years ago, and they're full of quartz, and the gold is in the quartz. They found a couple of nuggets when they were panning yesterday and realized it had to be coming from the canyon, so we rode up there this morning, and they think they found it – Lasseter's Reef.'

'What sized nuggets?' Jake narrowed his eyes, making some calculations in his head. If there were enough gold here to make them rich, if it turned out to be Lasseter's Reef, then he would never have to work again, never have to steal from anyone or risk his life with any crime that would put him back on the police radar. When his father had taken him through the outback in childhood, they had often panned for gold in creeks or fossicked for opals and dreamed of how life would be on 'easy street' if they struck it rich. Gold fever was already burning in his veins.

Dane tried to recall reports of gold finds that had made it to the news on television so that he could describe something believable, but the sound of galloping hooves broke his concentration. Everyone turned to see Days and Nu-man bolting into camp, desperate to be back with their friends after taking fright in the creek. For one terrifying instant, it looked as though the men were going to shoot the loose horses without question.

A scream caught in Lani's throat as she saw the guns aimed at the horses - she could not bear to see another horse die today. Then they seemed to realize the riderless horses posed no threat, and they did not attempt to stop Lani when she stepped forward to grab the reins as the two horses slid to a halt near their friends.

'You stay where you are,' Jake ordered the boys as Lani soothed Days and Nu-man with a gently crooning voice. 'Those your parents' horses?'

'Yes,' Lani lied smoothly, a worried expression on her face. She did not have to fake concern. With the body of her horse lying nearby and her cousin's and friend's horses arriving unexpectedly, she was genuinely concerned about what was going on. 'They must have broken out of their holding yard up the canyon.'

'It'll take hours for Mum and Dad to walk back from there,' added Dane, wondering what Brandon and Amy were doing. From the sand on Day's face, sides, and saddle, he guessed that he had fallen. Was Amy injured? Was she lying in the sandy bottom of the creek with Brandon trying to keep her alive? He was sure they would not have deliberately released their horses.

Scenarios and possibilities raced each other through his

mind as he tried to stay one step ahead of the escapees. His father's voice continued inside his head, telling him how to make a difficult horse do what you wanted: don't force him, don't tell him he has to do this or that, and give him choices. Make it easy for him to choose what you want him to do by making the other choices less favorable.

If the men thought they had hours before the adults came back to camp, the best choices open to them were to either leave the children tied up and leave immediately or, if the greed for gold had taken over, they might want to venture up the gorge. If they tried to leave and Gertie wouldn't start, they could either take the truck or maybe take it as a sign that they were meant to go looking for gold, and they'd want to go up the gorge.

Dane hoped that he had provided choices that were more inviting than killing them, which is what Meat favored. Put the choices in front of them and let them choose, he heard his father telling him, then work with what they give you. He lowered his eyes so that they would not have any hint at the myriad of thoughts galloping through his mind. He wanted to appear a frightened fourteen-year-old, not a calculating teen.

If the men chose to tie them up and leave, and Gertie refused to start - which he knew she would - he'd tell them to take the truck and hope that they would not want to take them as hostages. If they took the truck, he, Lani, and Matthew could wait for Amy and Brandon to arrive and untie them. Then, they could ride for help. If they chose to go looking for the gold, they would need the children to guide them, and they would need their hands free to negotiate the rough path they would follow into the gorge. The three Winters were at home in the heart of the Sunhaven Hills, and something deep inside told him they would be safe in the embrace of their land, a place that would be unfamiliar and hostile to men who were alien to this place.

If they wanted to see the gold, he would take them to the Galaxy Walk. If they could arrive before sundown, the reflections created from the last rays of the day would convince them that there was gold in the hills. If they arrived after dark, the torchlight on the walls would be even more impressive. It would be easier to escape from men who were distracted by a canyon full of gold than from men who were watching them like hawks.

Matthew coughed and looked so pointedly at his sister that Dane knew he was trying to communicate something. For an instant, he glanced at Lani, seeing her drawn face and sad eyes as she patted the two new arrivals, her gaze deliberately avoiding Fleet. He realized that Matty did not mean for him to look at Lani; it had to be something else, so, with his head turned slightly towards his sister, his eyes quickly scanned around and then dropped to his feet. Without pausing for a split second, his eyes had passed over the two figures by the creek. He raised his left hand to rub his eye, signaling *I see you* to them so discreetly that the men would not notice, but he knew Brandon would recognize it.

Staring at his shoes, he felt hope rise inside his chest. Amy and Brandon were nearby, and though they could not ride out to alert the police, he knew they would be able to help them somehow. As long as they could convince the men that they were worth more alive than dead, they could get out of this.

'So we tie the kids up?' Meat grunted, thinking about the hours it would take for their parents to walk back to camp. He did not mind shooting them as killing meant little to him, but he could see Jake's reasoning in wanting to avoid killing them. Everyone hated child killers - if they went back to prison, the other inmates would make their life hell. Child killers were not welcome in a place where many men were fathers, but he did enjoy killing. 'Maybe take one of 'em with us? We'll be long gone by the time they get back here.'

'Maybe,' Jake mused, preoccupied with thoughts of gold. What if it was there? How much did the kid's parents want it? Enough to share some of it and keep quiet about the escaped prisoners so that they could keep the rest? He wasn't sure about the laws regarding finding gold, but he imagined that if they revealed their discovery, they could lose it or have a lot of other people coming forward to make a claim. He smiled to himself. He had them: if they called the police, he would tell everyone about their gold: checkmate. They would have to keep quiet about the escapees if they wanted to keep their gold to themselves.

He began to see a glimmer of a plan emerging that could mean a happy ending for everyone. In his plan, there was no need to kill the kids or their parents, no need to worry about them calling the cops, and no need to think of ways to earn money in the future. If this was Lasseter's Reef, then there was enough for everyone. If he knew anything about the nature of humans, these people would keep everything a secret so that they would not risk losing their treasure.

'Where did you say your parents were?' Jake nodded at Dane.

'In Sunhaven Gorge,' Dane replied sullenly, 'there's a place they call the Galaxy Walk. They took us there this morning, then sent us back here so they could work out how much gold there is. They'll probably still be there or even further in the gorge. They reckon it's full of gold.'

Jake narrowed his eyes, thinking hard. Drive away now, or go for the gold. Either way, there was a good chance these people were not going to call the cops because they had too much to lose.

'Whatdya reckon?' he asked the other two men, looking from one to the other.

''Bout what?' Skinner asked. He had not been following the conversation all that closely. Long ago, he had found that it was easier to let Jake do all the thinking.

'The gold,' Jake tried not to roll his eyes at the stupidity of his offsider. 'What do you think about the gold? Is it worth trying to get a share?'

'I thought you said we shouldn't kill any more people,' Skinner looked a little puzzled, trying to understand what Jake had in mind.

'That's the beauty of it,' Jake smiled fox-like at him. 'We've got these gold fossickers out here with a big secret that they don't want anyone to know. My take on it is that they'll be so desperate to keep their secret, they'll let us have a bit and go on our way, and they're not going to tell anyone about us. If they're smart, they'd rather share some with us than risk losing most in a gold rush if the location was made public. '

'So, what's their secret?' Skinner asked, narrowing his eyes in thought as he tried to keep up with Jake's thinking.

'Gold,' Jake explained, less than patiently. 'They've discovered gold, and people who find gold don't want anyone else to know about it.'

'So,' Meat frowned as everything clicked into place in his brain, 'you reckon that even if they know about us, they won't tell the police?'

'Exactly,' Jake nodded. 'If we don't do any more than take their old bomb of a car and a little bit of their gold, what's that compared to keeping the secret about millions of dollars worth of gold? That's what Lasseter's Reef could be worth. They won't want the police here. They won't want any attention from anyone. As long as their kids are safe, they're not going to care about three blokes on the run. Got me?'

Although Dane hoped they would choose to leave, he also worried about what would happen when Gertie would not start. A trip up Sunhaven Gorge had the potential for action. It gave them the home ground advantage, and the coming night would also assist them. Having Brandon and Amy following along behind added to their chances, though he wanted to give them an idea of what they were playing at and where they were going.

The zip ties vanished into pockets, and the three Winters were allowed to stand with their horses while the men discussed traveling to the gorge. Jacke occasionally asked Dane questions about how far it was and how long it would take to get there.

'So, put those horses away and take us there,' Jake suddenly grinned at Dane as though they were friends. 'Seems like we're going into the gold business with your parents.'

Wanting to keep at least two horses with them, Dane nodded at him, 'I don't suppose you ride, do you? It's a lot quicker on horses.'

'Not a chance,' sniffed Jake. 'I know a bit about them, but I like my feet on the ground.'

'That's a shame,' Dane turned and began to lead Misty to the yards, 'Mum and Dad don't like them much, either. They wanted them for carrying the gold. If you have twenty kilos or more of something to carry, it's handy having pack horses to do the carrying.'

'Bring two of them,' Jake changed his mind as he looked at the sturdy saddlebags and imagined them filled with gold. 'Make sure the straps on those saddlebags are good and strong.'

Meeting her older brother's eyes, Lani knew that he would want to take Days and Misty as they were the two biggest and fastest horses in the group, and they could both carry two riders with ease if necessary. She handed him Days' reins and took Nu-man to the yards along with Shandy.

'Should we leave them a note or something?' Dane asked Jake, looking at him earnestly as though they were on the same side. 'In case they come back a different way, and we miss them, and then they get here to find us gone and your gear in Gertie? If they have a panic about that, they might go to the homestead down the road for help.'

The idea had merit, so Jake found some paper in the gooseneck and handed it to Dane, warning him to write carefully.

Hi Mum and Dad, he wrote, *if you get back here and we're gone, we're at the Galaxy Walk looking for you. Some men dropped in as their car broke down. We said they could take our car, but they want to pay you for it, so we're going to find you. It's OK; they know about the gold and said they wouldn't tell anyone. Dane.*

Handing it to Jake, Dane watched him closely as he read it, but there was no suspicion in his expression.

'What will they think if they see the dead horse?' Skinner scratched his head, looking at Fleet.

'Yeah, that is a problem,' Jake frowned.

Dane shook his head, 'Not really. I'll just say that Fleet broke his leg, and we had to put him down. That's just what you do when horses break their legs.'

Jake nodded thoughtfully. 'That should work. Add that.'

Dane wrote the extra sentence then handed the note back.

'Looks OK,' said Jake. 'Leave it where they'll see it, and let's get going.'

'Bit eager, eh?' Meat asked him, grinning.

'Lasseter's Reef, man,' Jake gave him a soft punch in the arm and smiled wolfishly. 'You can't imagine how much gold there'll be if that's what they've found.'

A click, whirr, and silence came from Gertie as Skinner leaned in the open window and turned the key for the first time since they started her when they first arrived. He tried again with the same result. Several more attempts followed, all with the click, whirr, and silence.

'Looks like the car's dead, anyhow,' Skinner kicked the door of the car angrily and glared at the children, his countenance making it clear that he'd be happy to shoot them now. 'So there'd better be some gold in those hills to make up for it.'

'I've seen it,' Dane assured him, lying smoothly, setting off at a walk leading Misty.

Lani followed, leaning on Days' neck as she walked, closing her eyes and letting the horse guide her steps. As security, Jake had ordered Matthew to walk with him, making it clear to the other two that he would die if they tried anything. Bringing up the rear, Meat and Skinner trudged awkwardly, their feet more used to city pavements and prison floors than this rough ground.

The late afternoon heat shimmered over the hills as they made their way towards Sunhaven Gorge. The Winters did not know what waited ahead, but they felt that the hills were calling them to safety. Their steps lightened as they approached the gorge while the footfalls of the men grew heavier.

CHAPTER TWELVE
Amy and Brandon
4 pm – 7 pm

'What are they doing?' Amy whispered up to Brandon, who was watching the camp from the top of the creek bank.

'Looks like they're going for a walk.'

'What?' she asked, crawling up the bank to lie beside him.

'They're going for a walk.'

They watched the group move away from the campsite as possible explanations went through their minds.

'You don't think they're going to kill them?' Amy looked at him, worried.

'Nah,' he shook his head, 'Why take the horses for that? Maybe Gertie wouldn't start again, and Dane told them there's a better car further over that way, and they're going to get it.'

For several minutes they tossed around ideas but could not come up with a reasonable explanation for why they had left the camp with two horses. When they were sure that the group wasn't returning, they climbed out of the creek and ran to the back of the gooseneck. Hiding behind it, they peeked around the end of it at the figures headed towards the hills. They looked at each other and shrugged.

'I have absolutely no idea what they're doing,' Amy narrowed her eyes, trying to work out what was going on. 'I can't see any reason why they'd walk off into the paddock.'

Brandon slid around to the front of the truck to check the two-way radio. Someone had pulled it out of its recess, and wires were sticking out everywhere, so he knew it was not going to be of any use. As Amy went to check on Numan and Shandy, he went to the door of the gooseneck and found Dane's note stuck there. He smiled as he read it, understanding the message perfectly. The men believed there were two adults out there, and they thought there was gold, so they wanted a share of it. Also, they were going down the gorge where home ground advantage went against the men.

'The horses seem fine,' Amy reported, omitting any mention of Fleet who lay nearby, his head in a congealing pool of blood. 'I don't know why they took Days and Misty, though.'

'I do,' Brandon held out the note for her to read. 'They think they're taking pack horses to carry gold. Dane must have told them that the Galaxy Walk was full of gold.'

Amy nodded. It made sense to her. If the men wanted to kill her cousins, they would at least wait until they had found the gold. The Winters were buying time.

'If we'd brought a gun with us, I could get up in the hills and pick them off,' Brandon mused.

'Do you really think you could kill people? It's not like shooting pigs or roos.'

'I think I could if it meant saving the lives of my friends.'

'Just as well Aunt Eleanor didn't let us bring a gun then,' she said. 'I could see a total disaster happening with bullets going everywhere in the gorge. The first shot would probably make them kill one of my cousins as a message to stop shooting.'

'They're going up the gorge – that's our territory,' Brandon raised his brows speculatively, ignoring her lecture on the dangers of shooting. He didn't know what they would do, but he knew they would come up with something. 'Let's get some stuff together and get going so we can get in front of them.'

'Is there any way we could signal someone, like with a fire or something?'

'If you don't mind risking killing a few thousand sheep, cattle, and horses, you're welcome to start a fire, but look at the grass around here – once a fire gets going, there's nothing to stop it,' Brandon extinguished that idea. 'The two-way was our best chance, and it's been totaled. You could probably take Shandy and head back to Sunhaven, if you wanted, and leave me to follow these guys.'

'I've thought of it,' she turned her green eyes on him, 'but what if I fall again? What if it takes too long for the police to get here and they decide to kill them? I keep feeling that it's wrong to stay and wrong to go.'

'Toss a coin,' he suggested as he climbed into the gooseneck and threw out a twenty-cent coin from the cutlery drawer. 'Heads, you stay with me.'

While he continued looking through the ransacked living area for anything that he might be able to use, Amy tossed the coin, slapping it down on the back of her hand, revealing the head of Queen Elizabeth.

'I'm staying with you. What will I need?'

'No idea,' he shrugged. 'I'm just thinking of anything that could be handy. Matches, a torch, some string, a knife.

Look – the UFO kites!' He held up the two kites with their attached LED lights. 'If they're in the canyon when it's dark, we might be able to use these to distract them.'

'Scare the diddlies out of them, more likely,' Amy took them from him and turned them over, examining the system of lights her cousins had glued there. 'Maybe if they're scared enough, it will make it easier for the others to get away from them.'

'Do you reckon Dane will be telling them about the Min Min lights in case we come up with something like the UFO kites?'

'Maybe,' Amy tried to imagine what her cousins were telling the men. She was sure Dane would string them along with stories to soften them up for whatever she and Brandon could plan. 'We know he's told them about gold and their parents, and I think he'll tell them about the Min Min, at least, he will if they see our fake Min Min. Maybe we won't get to see them this trip, but perhaps we might get to *be* them.'

Brandon gave her a quick smile, appreciating her line of thought. 'Good thinking.'

They collected some more items from the truck and gooseneck, leaving Gertie's load alone so the men would not realize that someone had visited the camp if they returned. Leaving the saddles and bridles where they were, they put headstalls and leads on the horses - gear the men were not likely to miss if they came back. After staging a breakout by pushing through the temporary yard fences to break them and make it appear as if the horses had left on their own accord, they tied the leads onto the headstalls to act as reins and vaulted on board. Brandon rode Nu-man and Amy took Shandy while the ever-faithful Blaze trotted at their heels.

With a last look around the campsite, they clicked the

horses into a canter and headed for the hills, aiming to climb to the top rather than follow the others up the canyon. They rode easily, swaying with the movement of their horses, the rope reins loose as the horses strode out strongly with Shandy leading. Now and then, Amy glanced back over her shoulder to check with Brandon about their direction, and he'd motion with his head or hand about veering left or right or continuing straight ahead. The horses' hooves kicked up dust as they cantered, but the breeze was so light that it did not raise the dust high enough to be seen by the men. Amy was sure even if they did see it, her cousins would explain it away as dust from cattle or sheep.

When they reached the lower slopes, they steadied the horses back to a walk. The day was still hot, and though the horses weren't sweating heavily, they knew it was because the dry air was absorbing the moisture from their coats as soon as it left their skin. They found a small soak halfway up the slope and paused to have a drink themselves before giving their horses access to the water. When they'd finished, Blaze dropped into the water and drank as he lay in it. For a few minutes, they led the horses to allow their backs to dry out where they'd been sitting, then they remounted and continued upwards, winding between the scrubby trees and rocks as the faint trail led them to the top. In the roughest places, they slowed to a walk, trotting, and cantering where possible.

'Do you know how to get to the Galaxy Walk from up here?' Amy asked as they walked side by side up the last of the slope, leaning forward over their horses' necks to give their hind legs the freedom to bound up the final steep incline.

'Not really,' he shook his head. 'I've never had to find it from up here, but it shouldn't be hard to pick. Just ride along the hills until we think we're as far along as we walked yesterday, then cut over to the canyon and have a look.'

'Sounds fair,' she nodded, 'I hope they are going there.'

'Dane wouldn't have named it if they weren't. We have to get there before them, and these horses are making that fairly easy. I'd reckon Dane, Lani, and Matthew will try and time it to arrive there about sundown in…' He glanced at his watch and saw it was getting close to five, '… a bit over two hours. Sunset is about seven. We should get there in another half hour at this pace, so that will give us an hour and a bit to prepare something.'

'I don't know what, though,' she sighed.

'Nup, no idea yet, but the UFO kites should be useful.'

'Is there a path from the top to the canyon floor so we can go down, or they can come up?'

'I haven't used it, but Dane mentioned a track yesterday, just the other side of the Galaxy Walk. If they escape, I bet they'll head there.'

'Let's hope we can come up with something that gives them the chance to get away.'

They rode on in silence, the afternoon sun cutting across their faces as it glided down towards the horizon. They could not know what the others were planning, but they could guess that they intended to escape from the men once they were distracted by the 'gold' and either use the horses to ride out of the gorge or go to the path which led to the top. Brandon knew they'd have to signal that they were at the top of the gorge, but he had an idea for that once they had taken up their position.

When he finally indicated to change direction and head towards the gorge, they found that they were halfway along the Galaxy Walk, with the sunlight touching the top section of the walls creating the sparks of fire that gave the section its name. For several seconds they sat staring at the myriad of crystals reflecting the light.

'Let's hope it will distract the men enough so that Dane, Matty, and Lani can get away,' said Amy.

'Between all that shining gold, the UFO kites, and whatever else we come up with, I think we'll be able to cause enough chaos to allow them to escape.'

'Maybe the real Min Min lights will help us,' Amy said, less than hopefully, 'they did help me that night I rode to Uncle John's place.'

'Maybe they will,' Brandon glanced around at the unusual rock formations that formed this part of the hills. He had never seen the Min Min lights himself, but he'd heard enough reports to believe that they existed, though whether they were balls of gas, lightning balls, or Dreamtime creatures was beyond him. They were something, and this area was unique enough to imagine that the Min Min could live here. He shivered. It was not just the unusual look of this spot, he thought; it *felt* different today.

'If you can take the horses,' he slid off Nu-man and handed the lead up to Amy, 'and find a spot a bit further along, well back from the canyon, I'll head back along the edge until I see where the others are. Stay with the horses, though. I might be a while.'

'We've already found out the hard way that Nu-man can spook and take off,' Amy rubbed the horse on the forehead as he rested his chin on Shandy's neck. 'No offense, boy, but we'd prefer you to stay with us this time.'

'If you hold them for a while to make sure they're settled, you should be able to tie them up. Shandy's a placid fellow. He'll keep Nu-man calm.'

'And then wait here for you?'

Brandon nodded, then turned and took off at a run, his

feet flying across the rock-strewn path made by goats and kangaroos along the edge of the gorge. After a few minutes, he slowed to an easy jog that he could keep up for hours if needed, but he predicted he'd catch sight of the others within half an hour. He was fairly sure Dane would be trying to time their arrival at the Galaxy Walk with sundown so that the end-of-day shadows would help them, which would mean that they would be making their way slowly along the canyon floor.

He spotted them easily, two horses and six people winding along the gorge like miniature toys that he could reach down and pick up between fingertips. So far away, he thought as he looked at them, and yet we have to be able to save them from up here.

They had already passed the Sun Pools, and he wondered if they pretended it was difficult to have Misty and Days jump up the rock ledge. It would have given the Winters another opportunity to delay the journey to get their timing right. As he'd thought, Dane was well in the lead, moving slowly, with Lani following twenty or more paces behind as though Dane had told her to remain well back. Brandon smiled to himself. He knew Dane would have organized it that way so that he could receive signals from above if any came. Growing up playing their war games together, they'd always valued the high ground, so Dane would know that his friend would head there.

Matthew was back with the men, well behind his brother and sister - their guarantee of good behavior from the others, Brandon guessed. He and Amy would have to come up with a plan that enabled all the Winters to escape as he knew Lani and Dane would not leave without their little brother.

From his pocket, he took a small mirror and waited several minutes until Dane turned a slight bend in the canyon. He grabbed the sunlight on its surface and sent it down to the canyon wall in front of Dane. For half a minute, he estimated, Dane would be the only one who could see it, and Brandon worked quickly to bounce the spot of light in front of him in a Morse pattern: -... --- - .... ..- .--. .... . .-. . *both up here.*

Dane held his right arm out in front of him and gave a thumbs-up sign only visible from in front and above. The rest of the group began making their way around the bend, and Brandon pocketed the mirror. At least Dane knew where they were.

He headed back to Amy and found her sitting on a rock at the far end of the Galaxy Walk, looking at the items they'd brought with them, puzzling over how they could use them. As he approached, Blaze looked up and wagged his tail, whining a soft welcome. The horses were standing calmly, tied well back from the edge of the canyon, so there was little chance of them hearing the other horses below and calling to them.

'Looks like Dane is walking slow so that we can expect them just on dark,' he told her. 'They all look OK so far. The men are keeping Matty with them. I'd say they've made it clear to Dane and Lani that Matty will pay if they get up to anything.'

'So we have to make sure he doesn't pay,' said Amy, her eyes bright with anger at the thought of them harming her youngest cousin. 'Let's get planning. I have some ideas.'

HORSES OF THE LIGHT

CHAPTER THIRTEEN
Sundown

The floor of the gorge had been deep in shadows for the last few hours of the afternoon. The only light came from the line of sunlight across the top of the eastern wall and from the sky itself. Above, it appeared as though the dark fabric of the canyon walls had been ripped open to reveal a bright blue sky atop the gloom. The temperature was plummeting. The heat of summer could not keep the canyon warm once the direct sunlight was gone, and the shifting air temperatures caused the cooler air to flow along the canyon to the lowest places.

Lani looked ahead at Dane's back, his shoulders dimly lit by the narrow strip of sky above, and shivered. It was not just the cool air down here. It wasn't only the fact that the three men behind them could kill them - it was this place. Sunhaven Gorge was like the sacred heart of her land. Her father had always told her to respect the soul of the canyon, and walking into it with guns and the prospect of violence felt so very wrong.

Shaking her head, she muttered a whispered apology to

the land for their intrusion and asked for help. A sudden gust of warm air hit her face as though in reply, and she looked around, startled. She could have sworn she caught a hint of her father's aftershave on the air. Looking back, she saw Matthew staring around the shadow world as though he had sensed something, too.

'Hey, kid!' Jake called to Dane. 'How much further?'

'Not far now,' Dane replied, pointing ahead and up at the top of the canyon walls where the last of the day's light played on the eastern rim. 'Another bend or so, and you'll see the gold shining in the rock up there.'

'No sign of your parents,' grumbled Meat suspiciously.

'Once the horses escaped, they could have walked back to camp another way,' Lani pointed out, 'or they could still be further ahead. If they began digging gold out of the canyon walls, they're not likely to walk away.'

'And there's a full moon tonight,' Dane pointed out. 'When the moon is high enough, they'll be able to see down here without torches and go on digging. You don't know how obsessed they are when it comes to gold.'

Jake nodded, satisfied by their explanation. If he found a reef of gold, he would be reluctant to leave it. He eyed the deepening shadows all around as the darkness claimed the canyon, 'We should have bought torches with us.'

Dane turned away and smiled grimly. He had been glad that the men had not thought to bring torches. It would help them when it came time to escape as darkness and shadows would be their friends. 'The moon will be up soon,' he told Jake, 'it won't be that dark, then.'

'Yeah, just as well,' Skinner uttered a curse as he stumbled on a rock. 'It shouldn't be this dark yet. It's not even seven o'clock.'

'Do your parents have guns or anything like that with them?' grunted Meat, worried that they could turn a corner and find themselves face to face with a family firing squad.

'We don't believe in guns,' replied Dane. 'I can call ahead if you'd like to try and let them know that we're coming, and you mean no harm. It isn't far to the Galaxy Walk now.'

Jake considered the pros and cons of this suggestion. He decided that if the boy could make his parents feel comfortable about their approach, it would be better than if they suspected escaped criminals were coming along the gorge with their children.

'No tricks, though,' Jake growled at him. 'Don't you doubt for a moment that we'd kill one or all of youse if we felt like it.'

'No tricks,' Dane promised calmly, 'I'll tell them that we're coming with friends if that's OK with you. I don't want my parents getting shot, or us for that matter. If they're still in the Galaxy, they'd probably like to know that we're about to arrive.'

With a brief nod, Jake cleared it with Dane, who immediately put his hand to his mouth and shouted, 'Hey, Mum! Dad! Are you there? We're coming, and we have some friends with us.'

The echoes bounced back at them, but no other noises. Dane repeated his call.

They had stopped to listen for an answering voice when the unearthly wail that had frightened them yesterday came racing down the canyon at them. Even though yesterday, they had convinced themselves that it was a curlew, it still made Dane, Lani, and Matthew uneasy. The men, hearing the sound for the first time, stared around nervously. The horses threw their heads up and skittered backward, snorting in fear.

'What the hell!' Skinner stared into the darkness ahead and cursed several times, his eyes wide.

'Explain,' Jake barked at Matthew, the hairs on the back of his neck standing up as the wail died away.

'The Min Min,' Matthew looked at them, recognizing the primal fear in their eyes. He nodded knowingly, feigning fear as he widened his eyes.

'Min Min?' Meat asked.

'The Min Min lights live here,' said Lani, trying to put a quiver of terror into her voice. 'Well, they're supposed to. Perhaps they guard the gold. Some people think they're aliens or ghosts. Others think they are the souls of the dead. They could be just swamp gas or something. But they abduct people. Every year someone goes missing around these parts. We don't believe the stories, but people disappear when the Min Min cry.'

'Just made up rubbish,' Jake spat. 'They're not real. They're made up tales about lights.'

The canyon walls once more rang with the haunting call that chilled those who heard it.

'Why haven't your parents answered?' Skinner's voice stuttered as he spoke.

'Maybe they didn't hear us,' Dane suggested, looking nervous as he edged closer to the others, discreetly shaking Misty's reins to make her jiggle around restlessly. 'They could have gone right to the far end of the canyon, but funny things happen here, so who knows where they are.'

'What sort of funny things?' Skinner asked.

'Noises, lights, that sort of thing,' Dane signaled for Misty to back up and followed her as though trying to calm her down. 'Horses go a bit crazy in here, like this. That's probably why the horses bolted out this afternoon – they get terrified of something here.'

'I reckon we should get outa here,' Skinner turned to Jake. He had always been a superstitious person, believing in good luck charms and curses, and this canyon felt as though it was placing a curse on his head.

'Horses get frightened of anything,' Jake told him. 'Shadows frighten them. That noise was probably just a dingo or a bird, so eat some cement, and let's keep going. I want to see that gold.'

Convinced they had sewn the seeds of fear in fertile soil, Dane, Lani, and Matthew glanced at each other. The apprehensive expressions that the men saw on their faces in the faint light differed from the calm resolution in the eyes that met each other. *We will get out of this*, they said to each other as clearly as if they had spoken the words aloud. Where the cry of the curlew, or whatever animal it was, had scared them yesterday, now it merely reminded them that they were in their land and these men were the intruders.

They continued, slower than before as the dying of the day made it difficult to see the trail.

Meat and Skinner found their legs more reluctant to walk into the canyon after the unearthly cry had shaken their nerves. Matthew tried to walk slightly further ahead with his brother and sister, but Jake put a firm hand on his shoulder and told him to stay close. He wasn't sure how the parents of these children would greet them, so he wanted to keep the boy within reach in case he needed him as a hostage. A gun to the head of a loved one usually had the desired result in controlling people.

The men looked in surprise as a faint glow that ran the full height of the canyon could be seen ahead, past the shadows. They didn't see the pleased looks that passed between the children - they had timed it perfectly. The men were about to be treated to the full effects of the Galaxy Walk at sunset.

Stumbling around the next corner, the men stopped, their faces frozen in awe at the sight of the last rays of sunlight hitting the crystals at the top of the eastern canyon wall. The light shattered into a billion pieces and cascaded down both walls as the crystals caught the light, broke it up, and sent it on its way. It looked, for those last few minutes of the day, as though the canyon was made entirely of glittering gold.

While the men stared in wonder at the golden walls, Dane, Lani, and Matthew looked at the footing ahead through the Galaxy Walk. They knew there weren't many minutes before the sun's touch left the walls, and darkness would wrap around them. It would be some time before the moon would be high enough to cast her light on them. They needed to be sure of where they could run when they had the chance.

Using small movements of his fingers and eyes, Dane indicated that Lani was to get on Days and ride. He would grab Matthew and follow on Misty. He narrowed his eyes to slits to start adjusting his eyes to the dark that was about to strike. Matthew and Lani copied him. They needed to get their pupils dilated, so they could see better than the wide-eyed men who were gazing at the light.

'It really is Lasseter's Reef,' Jake spoke in hushed tones, suitably stunned by what he was seeing. A canyon made of gold.

Meat and Skinner swore in astonishment at the sight and then grinned at each other. Before they could go forward to dig their fingers into the canyon walls to try and claw out some of the gold, the sun sank lower, leaving just a fragment of light on the ridge of crystal at the top, and the golden light drained away. Within seconds the remarkable glow was extinguished by the dark. Dane nodded to Lani.

In one fluid movement, Lani flicked the reins over Days' head and vaulted onto his back, pushing him straight into a gallop across the sand and stones as she leaned forward over his neck. The horse didn't hesitate or stumble. He was determined not to fall with another rider that day, and he listened to every light aid she gave him as she guided him around the rocks.

As Lani leaped onto Days, Dane turned to lunge at Matthew and grabbed him out of Jake's hands. With Matthew taking several huge bounds, Dane swung him past himself and launched him up onto Misty's back where he clung like a monkey, bracing against the mare's neck as Dane swung up behind him. It was a move they had practiced many times at pony club as they played various games involving two people on the one horse. Misty, keen to follow Days, surged forward with her two riders as gunshots exploded next to her. The explosions, magnified by the narrow walls of the canyon, hammered at Misty's ears, and she swerved in surprise.

Jake had recovered quickly and was already shooting at the fleeing Lani, his anger ignited by their attempt to escape. It was too dark to see clearly, but he could see the shape of the horse and rider in the gloom. He sent several bullets down the canyon at them, rewarded by the dull *thunk* of a bullet striking flesh. He didn't care if he hurt or killed the horse or the girl. Once his temper was fired up, he had no thought of consequences, only the burning need to lash out.

Realizing that the second horse had shied at his gunshots and had unbalanced the two boys, he dived forward before they could straighten up and follow their sister. He collided with Misty's rump as she spun around with Dane pulling on one rein, trying to haul himself upright. Reaching blindly, he grabbed a leg and hauled back, pulling both boys off the horse and onto the sand. He threw himself on top of them and forced their heads down while yelling to Meat and Skinner to help him.

'Stupid kids,' he cursed at them once he stood and dusted himself off, leaving his two offsiders to hold Matthew and Dane while he held Misty's reins. 'I shot your sister, d'ya hear me?' He raised his voice to a shout and shook his gun at them. 'It's your fault. Your parents would have shared the gold with us. There's enough for everyone. You didn't have to go and do something stupid like this!'

Dane hung his head. They did have to do something, he thought. Once the men realized there was no gold and no parents, they would only be angrier and more likely to kill them. He had heard the sound of the bullet hitting either Lani or Days, but since the horse had galloped on and he hadn't heard Lani call out, he hoped that it was just a flesh wound, and both were safe further up the gorge. Shooting almost blindly in the dark would have made them a hard target, and he wanted to believe that a fatal shot would have been unlikely.

'Now I know I can't trust you,' he snarled at them. 'So, first up, I'm gunna kill that horse of yours so you won't be thinking of trying to ride off again.'

'Please don't,' Dane breathed, his heart chilled. He couldn't bear the thought of losing his horse. 'It's not her fault. Just let her go, and she'll run away.'

Jake raised his gun and pointed the muzzle at Misty's forehead, his teeth flashing white in the gloom as he smiled coldly. 'You do the wrong thing, you get punished. That's life, boys.'

'Run, Misty!' Matthew wriggled out of Skinner's grasp and kicked sand at Misty, trying to make her take off. 'Get out of here! Go on! Get out of here!'

Misty snorted and pulled back from Jake, but he held tight to her reins. Pivoting on one foot to face Matthew, he raised his right hand and brought the gun down across the side of his face, knocking him to the ground. He took a step closer to Matthew's prone form and drew a foot back, ready to kick him, not caring that his strength could rupture the boy's organs.

'Leave him!' roared Dane, struggling futilely against the iron hold of Meat, who just laughed at his efforts. 'You'll kill him.'

'That's the idea,' laughed Meat in Dane's ear, excited by the violence.

'Shoulda thought of that before trying to run,' grunted Jake as he landed a boot in Matthew's stomach and sent his unconscious body rolling across the sand.

He followed and was about to kick him a second time when Dane screamed at him to stop, desperate to save his brother and frustrated by the arms that held him. 'He's only ten years old. Leave him alone! Fight me if you want, but not him.'

Meat tightened his hold on Dane's arms, twisting them back until the bones were almost breaking, but he continued to struggle and beg for Jake to stop the beating.

It wasn't Dane's voice that stopped him from delivering the kick, though; it was the string of swearing that erupted from Skinner.

'Look!' Skinner pointed up, his hand barely visible in the darkness.

In the blackness of the canyon floor, with only the faint light of the evening sky filtering down to provide a dim outline of the landscape, it was difficult to see where he was pointing, but the object of his attention easily caught their eyes. Two glowing lights hovered unsteadily high in the gorge further down the Galaxy Walk, like the glowing eyes of a giant cat looking down on them. Their green glow was unnatural, and the silence that held the canyon felt as though the land was holding its breath in awe of the sight.

'The Min Min!' gasped Dane.

The men swore and tried to blame the lights on a helicopter or plane, though their voices betrayed their doubts.

'It'll be the cops,' Skinner spoke in doomed tones. 'They found us. It'll be their chopper.'

'It's the Min Min,' repeated Dane. 'They're coming in silence. That's what they do. If it were a chopper, we'd hear it, but the Min Min hunt silently. Once their eyes are on you, they come for you.'

As the men stared at the lights, Dane felt Meat's hold on him loosen, and he tried to increase their fears of the Min Min.

'You gotta let us go,' he begged, an edge of hysteria carefully added to his voice. 'My brother and I don't want to be here with the Min Min. You don't know what they do to people.'

Despite the terror in his voice, he felt calm as he assessed the situation. Matthew had not moved from where he'd rolled, which scared him as Jake's blow to his head and follow-up kick had been brutal. Jake and Skinner had all their attention on the Min Min lights, and Meat's arms held him less firmly by the second. He couldn't run until he knew Matthew was able to come with him. He'd carry him if he had to.

Could I get him onto Misty's back? He looked from his brother to his horse but doubted he'd be strong enough to lift the dead weight of Matthew onto Misty and hold him there while controlling the horse.

Preoccupied with the menacing lights staring down at them, Meat loosened his grip on Dane. He almost stumbled to his knees as the burly arms let go and, though he could have escaped, he stayed as he would not leave Matthew. Looking up at the lights, he realized why Meat released him. The lights were moving from side to side, giving the impression of a snake's eyes weaving back and forth, focused on their prey before striking.

'They're coming for us,' Dane exhaled, watching the lights dip and sway, unable to get any perspective as to how far away they were.

Judging by the cursing from the men, they had no idea what the lights were, and, in the heavy silence of the gorge, Dane could sense their anxiety rising. Their attention was no longer on the boys or Misty but totally on the strange lights above. He had to admire the skills of Amy and Brandon as they worked the UFO kites, though he wasn't sure how they managed to have them flying side by side so perfectly when there didn't appear to be a breath of wind.

Amy and Brandon were not flying the kites. After signaling Dane with his mirror, Brandon had rejoined Amy, and they made their plans. While the ones below slowly approached the Galaxy Walk, Brandon had run along the gorge to the small bridge that spanned it near Legend's Leap, more than a kilometer away, and crossed to the other side. He was a champion cross country runner at school, and he needed all his skills and fitness to negotiate the rough country at speed.

When he'd arrived on the clifftop opposite Amy, she tied a stick to the end of one of the kite cords and, after swinging it around her head, launched it across to him. With them either side of the gorge, they were able to attach the kites and lights to the string and pull them back and forth, and dip them by loosening the string then tugging it tight to make them zoom back up.

Although they couldn't see down into the black pit that was the gorge at sundown, the acoustics of the canyon sent every whisper from the floor up to them, so they knew that Lani had already made her escape on Days. They also realized that a bullet had struck either Lani or Days. They knew one of the men had hit Matthew, and they hadn't heard his voice since the moment he told Misty to run, so they were worried he was injured. Matthew tended to be chatty, so silence from him was worrying.

Dane's words about the Min Min carried up to them. To reinforce the appearance of mythical lights, they increased the activity of the kites, lowering them further and pulling them back up quickly, knowing that they would look like impressive maneuvers from below.

Tying the end of his string to a tree, Brandon stood back from the edge so that no one could see him from below. He shone a torch on himself so that Amy could see him clearly in the last moments of twilight. He pointed to himself then at the track they had surveyed earlier that led down into the canyon, making a walking motion with his fingers in the torch beam to indicate that he was going down to the others. Following his lead, she fastened the end of her string around her hand, used her torch to illuminate herself. With hand signals, she asked if she should stay with the kites or follow down the path on her side. Raising a hand in a stop sign, he pointed to her, making it clear that she should stop there. They still had some tricks to play out, and she would have to undertake them alone.

Amy nodded and shone the torch on her hand as she gave him a thumbs-up sign, then went back to moving the kites around. With the remote control, she could switch the lights off, lower the kites down twenty meters before they hit the far side of the canyon, then turn them back on and pull them up quickly. The display of drop, lift, and lights on and off was not as effective as when they each had an end of the string, but it still appeared as though the Min Min lights were thinking of attacking those below.

There had been no more hoof falls from Days, so Amy

had no idea what had happened to him and Lani. She had heard him pass by below and head further into the canyon, then nothing. Either they had continued on soft grass that muffled the sounds of their steps, or they had stopped. She didn't want to think of her horse or her cousin injured or dying, but she knew it was a possibility. She was glad Brandon was going down to find them. She had faith that he would know how to help them.

As she stared into the blackness below, she closed her eyes and uttered a fervent prayer for the safety of her cousins, Brandon, and Days. She had no idea how the help could arrive, but she knew that, without it, it was unlikely that they would all survive the night with those men in the gorge.

****

Days stopped. When Lani collapsed off him and fell to the ground, he stopped and stood next to her, his head lowered as he breathed on her face. For a minute or so, Lani lay unmoving, biting her lip to stop crying out in pain from the bullet in her leg. When Days gently nudged her, she reached out and rubbed his forehead.

'I'll be OK, boy,' she whispered so softly that the sound would not carry further than his ears. 'It hurts a bit, but I'll be fine.'

As she saw the slick shine of her blood down Days' side, she wondered if she would be alright. That looked to be a lot of blood on him as well as what was soaking into the sand around her leg. Pushing a hand hard against the bleeding hole in her thigh, she whimpered from the searing agony of the bullet moving inside her leg, but she needed to staunch the flow of blood. She knew that the femoral artery had not been hit, or she would have already bled to death. That was something she had heard of before in the outback where it could take hours to get medical help. Still, she did not want to lose any more blood. It might not be until the next day, even longer, before she received help, and she needed to do all that she could to hang on until help came.

Until help came, her shoulders shrugged in half despair, half amusement at her thoughts. What help? What could Brandon and Amy do against three men with guns? Perhaps Amy had taken one of the horses from the campsite and ridden for help. Maybe she had reached Sunhaven and called the police, but no one would find them before morning. They were deep in the heart of their land, out of reach of anyone who could help, in the home of the Min Min. Her thoughts began to wander as she thought of her father who said this is where he would go when he died, the heart of the land, the Galaxy Walk, the stairway to the stars.

'Looks like I might be joining you, Daddy,' she whispered to the air, a sensation of lightness taking over her mind, 'but maybe you could help the others get out alive. This is your place. You always said it was, so are you here, Daddy? Where are you?'

She closed her eyes and slid away from consciousness into the welcoming embrace of dreams. A breath of air pushed against her face, and she caught the faint fragrance that her father had used. She looked up and smiled.

****

The players were all in place. Matthew unconscious on the sand. Dane standing by the three men wondering how he would get his brother away. Jake, Meat, and Skinner staring up at the Min Min lights that weaved menacingly overhead. Lani fighting to remain alive as the pain and shock overtook her while Days stood guard over her, his nose resting gently on her hair. Brandon finding his way down the goat track to the floor of the gorge, using his torch to find his footing since he knew the men couldn't see around the bend to where he was descending. Amy at the top of the gorge operating the fake Min Min lights and fumbling in the dark for matches. She and Brandon planned to light the strip of dry brush and grass that they had arranged for a hundred meters along the bare ground at the edge of the canyon where it could burn without setting fire to anything else.

They were all in place when the Min Min arrived.

HORSES OF THE LIGHT

CHAPTER FOURTEEN
The Arrival of the Min Min

The curlew cried out with the blood-curdling call that stilled hearts in the night, its cry echoing down the gorge so that it sounded as if dozens of Banshees were wailing for the dead. Even though Dane was positive the noise was from the little bird, he could not help the shiver that ran the length of his spine as he listened to it.

'They're calling to the souls of the dead,' he told the men in reverent tones. 'The Min Min are coming to take us. They are calling our souls away.'

'Shut up,' Jake growled at him, unable to see him clearly in the dark but no longer caring about his whereabouts. 'It's just a bird,' he told Meat and Skinner, 'don't listen to the boy.'

The curlew cried again.

'That ain't no bird,' Skinner said fearfully. 'I know what birds sound like, and that's no bird.'

Dane was kneeling next to his brother, his hands feeling over his skin for any protrusions that could signify broken bones. Nearby, Meat made a strangled cry and fell to his knees in the sand, whimpering like a scared dog. The light from the UFO kites must have grown brighter as Dane could now see Meat on his knees, his face a mask of pale dread, his hands clasped in front of him. *Praying!* He turned to see the faces of Skinner and Jake, upturned and frozen in terror, their lips moving but no sound coming out.

A breeze sprang up and ruffled Dane's hair. He turned his face into it and raised his eyes to the sky. Another pair of lights had joined the first two: a slightly different color, softer yet brighter without any distinct edge so that it was difficult to judge their distance. They floated in the air somewhere below and beyond the UFO kites, and Dane knew instantly that these were not the work of Brandon and Amy. These were the Min Min.

They began to sink slowly, lighting the walls as they dropped, sending out fragments of gold as the crystals in the cliffs caught the light and reflected it. Another pair of lights appeared out of the blackness and followed the first. A third pair blinked into existence. The glow from the six new lights radiated around the canyon, spreading visibility and causing the cliffs to become bejeweled in gold as the crystals lit up.

The sight that filled the men with dread had the opposite effect on Dane. He gazed at the lights in wonder, relief flooding his heart. He knew they had come to help. The Min Min were there to protect them, and he did not doubt that for a single moment as he looked at them gathering in the air of the Galaxy Walk. He, Matthew, and Lani belonged to the land, as did the Min Min, but the men came from the outside. They came with violence in their souls, and they did not respect this place. Anger flowed from the lights, as tangible as spears thrown at the men. Jake, Skinner, and Meat felt it and cowered.

Amy, busy at the top of the canyon looking for the

matches, had not seen the additions to the UFO kites. She focussed on starting the fire, which she hoped would provide enough confusion so her cousins could escape. Ignoring the soft whining of Blaze and without looking in the gorge, she struck a spark to the tinder-dry handfuls of grass they had placed under the sticks and branches and ignited the fire along the cliff edge. She watched the flames spread along their path of dried vegetation, casting flickering red light and shadows across the ravine. From below, the appearance of the fire should prove quite alarming as the blood-red light washed down the walls and danced with the shadows.

Only when the fire was well alight did she look down. She was stunned to see the lights hovering in formation below, slowly closing in on Dane, Matthew, and the men. The glowing orbs lit the figures at the bottom of the gorge. With a hand over her mouth, she stared down at the lights, tears pricking her eyes as she took in the ethereal beauty of the spheres.

On the night of the storm, when she had ridden over the hills to get help, Min Min lights had guided her down the path on the far side to Uncle John's house. They had been far ahead and could have been people with torches except for their floating movement. That night there were just two lights, but *eight* lights! No, ten. Another two appeared behind Dane and Matthew and floated in the air towards them.

Once more, the curlew cried, and that, combined with the Min Min and the fire that made the canyon look like the pits of hell, was too much for Skinner. Amy watched him turn and flee. He repeatedly fell as he panicked, trying desperately to escape the lights of the gorge and the rain of sparks from the fire above. Several pairs of lights detached from the main group and drifted slowly after him, their effortless, silent glide at odds with his scrambling, shrieking run.

Matthew lay unmoving with Dane kneeling next to him, protecting him from falling embers and ready to attack anyone else who might harm his brother, his eyes on the congregating orbs. The sparks that fell from the fire above passed right through them, he noticed, and though the Min Min were bright, they were completely transparent. He was able to see the red ashes as they fell through the orbs. They were light without substance; they had neither body nor eyes. There was no place where a brain could be stored, yet they behaved as though they were communicating with each other and had a plan. They were making decisions to target the men and leave him, Matthew, and Misty alone.

Amy ran along the top of the gorge, looking for Lani. By the light of the Min Min and the fire, she could see around the bend to where Days was standing watch over Lani. Her cousin sat with her back against a rock, staring up at several glowing points that appeared to be hovering over her. Days was not showing any sign of being disturbed by the presence of the lights. Lani stretched her right hand up to them as though reaching to take the hand of someone who was offering to help her stand. At Amy's side, Blaze stared down towards Lani, his tail wagging furiously, and he uttered little yips of excitement like he did when he saw her coming home.

'Shh, boy,' Amy patted him. 'I don't think there's anything we can do at the moment except sit and watch. I think they're going to be safe.'

More and more glowing spheres appeared out of the air of the canyon. There were dozens of them, all in pairs, floating along the gorge. Meat kneeled, praying for the first time in his adult life. Jake fumbled to load more bullets into his revolver, swearing as he dropped them into the sand.

Once loaded, he started firing, and Amy saw the flash of the gunfire moments before the sound of the reports reached her as he shot at the lights. He emptied the gun in seconds, then lunged over to Meat, grabbed his gun, and continued firing. The slow approach of the gathering Min Min did not falter in the face of bullets.

Brandon had stopped on the path halfway down the canyon walls, unable to see what was happening around the bend, but he knew the Min Min had arrived. A pair had floated over to him and brushed past so close that he could have touched them if he had merely raised his hand. He felt a ripple of light pass through him as though they weighed and measured him. He smiled at the sensation, and the Min Min passed on. It was now light enough in Sunhaven Gorge for him to see the path without the torch, but he felt as though he had been gently instructed to remain in this spot, so he waited.

Dane felt for Matthew's pulse: it was even and strong. He groaned slightly but did not open his eyes as Dane carefully picked him up and struggled to his feet, cradling his brother in front of him. He looked at Jake and Meat, but they posed no threat to him now as they stared at the lights that gathered around them, crowding in closer and closer, their eyes seeing something far more terrifying than what Dane beheld.

The Min Min showed no interest in Dane and his brother. They merely moved aside as he walked through them. With a quiet call to Misty, the horse walked up to him, surprisingly calm in the presence of so much supernatural activity. Calling for Misty to follow, he began walking up the canyon towards where he'd last seen their sister. The mare walked with him, her muzzle almost on his back. For a moment, he considered trying to put his brother on Misty's back, but he just held him closer. *He's my brother*, he thought, *I will carry him.*

The Min Min continued to collect around Jake and Meat as Dane walked away. He heard the clicking of the hammer of Jake's gun as it fell on empty chambers, and he did not look back. He needed to find Lani. Even when he heard the voices of the two men crying out at the lights, he did not turn around. It was business best left to the Min Min.

With his arms burning from the strain of carrying Matthew, he trudged through the Galaxy Walk, Misty at his back, their shadows cast far ahead of them by the lights behind. Barely noticing the brilliant fragments that bounced off the crystals in the walls around him, he walked on, over the sand and around the rocks, one foot after the other, Matthew's head rolling against his shoulder. When he rounded the bend in the canyon floor, it was darker and more difficult to see as all the Min Min were now behind him in the Galaxy Walk. He paused a moment to wrap Misty's reins around her neck, then clicked to make her walk ahead of him. He followed on her heels, trusting her to find the best path to Days and Lani.

Matthew groaned and moved in his arms.

'You right, Matty?' he gently asked.

'Is Misty OK?'

Dane grinned down at him, amused that his first words were for the horse and not himself. 'She's right in front of us, Matty; you saved her. Reach out, and you'll touch her tail.'

'I don't want to touch her smelly butt,' Matthew mumbled, prompting a snort from Dane. 'What about Lani?'

'We're going to find her now,' he squinted in the murky light, so different from the brightness of the crystal gallery behind them. 'I think I can see Days up ahead. Think you could ride Misty now?'

'Better than you.'

'In your dreams, bro.'

Dane called for Misty to halt. She stopped and patiently stood while he helped Matthew into the saddle. Once Matthew had the reins, they continued towards the faint, pale shape of Days several hundred meters away. After a few sickening screams and shrieks of terror from the men behind, there was silence. They looked around at the dark walls that reared up over them, aware only of the sound of their footfalls and the beat of their hearts.

'How'd we get away?' Matthew's spoke sotto voiced. As his head began to clear, he remembered trying to stop Jake from shooting Misty, but nothing beyond that.

'The Min Min,' Dane informed him. 'You slept through it all.'

He told Matthew about the UFO kites being used to distract the men and the gathering of the lights. Matthew chuckled when he described how Skinner ran while Meat prayed and Jake tried to shoot the Min Min.

'And I picked you up and left. They didn't seem to worry about you or me or Misty, so I thought we should get out of there while we could.'

'It sucks that I had to miss out on it and wake up with a sore head and bellyache.'

'Jake kicked you in the stomach,' Dane added some swear words directed at the coward for attacking his ten-year-old brother, 'that's why you're sore there. You'll probably have a fair sort of bruise coming up, but if the pain gets too bad, let me know in case it's worse than a bruise.'

'It just feels like some big bloke kicked me in the stomach,' Matthew grimaced in the dark. 'Were you scared when you saw the Min Min?'

Dane thought about this for a few seconds. It surprised

him that, after all the years of hearing frightening stories of the Min Min, the lights themselves had not inspired any terror in him. He felt as though they accepted him as much as the rocks and trees around them. He was another part of the land, and their interest lay with the intruders who brought brutality into their sanctuary. He recalled Amy saying she felt she could trust them when they guided her down to Uncle John's house. Now he understood what she meant.

'Nah,' he smiled to himself, 'they made me feel pretty safe, really.'

'Sucks that I missed them, then,' Matty scowled.

'They might be still around.'

Some pebbles tinked and tapped down the canyon wall next to them, and they looked up to see a light. For a moment, Matthew thought he had his chance to see them, but then the torch cut a beam down towards them.

'Glad you guys are OK,' Brandon's voice came from above.

'Thanks for the distraction back there,' Dane called back softly. Although he was fairly sure that the threat from the men had passed, he did not want to bring attention to their whereabouts in case they were free from whatever the Min Min had been doing and were looking for them. 'Good job with the UFO kites.'

'Those kites are cool,' said Matthew.

'No problem. Keep going,' said Brandon. 'It's not that much further to Lani. I'll be a few minutes yet as I'm trying not to fall and break my neck.'

'Good plan,' Dane grinned his approval, his teeth flashing white in the dark. Then he added, in a worried whisper that barely made its way up the cliff to Brandon, 'Is she OK, do you know?'

'Can't say,' Brandon huffed as he jumped from rock to

rock down the narrow path lit by his torch. He wanted to add something optimistic and amusing that would have his friends smiling, but he held fears for Lani's well-being and could not make light of the situation. 'Can't say,' he repeated unhappily.

Matthew clicked at Misty to get her moving again, and Dane walked beside them, one hand resting lightly on his brother's leg. The stars in the slash of sky above blazed brightly, but their light was not strong enough to illuminate the canyon floor, so Dane walked carefully, pushing his shoes across the top of the sand to make sure his next step would not have him falling. The full moon was rising and was already painting the top of the western canyon wall with her reflected brilliance. Dane looked up at the line of brightness that was climbing down the rocks as the moon rose higher in the east. Even though they could not see her yet, the moon gave them enough light to see the shapes of the rocks around them.

In the last twenty meters before reaching Lani, the light from the sky above was enough to make out her shape at the feet of the big horse. She sat with her back to the rock, her eyes closed, a look of utter peace on her face. Dane felt an icy fear grip his chest. As he broke into a run, he thought of how the Min Min were reputed to come and collect the souls of the dead. Had they taken Lani? Blood covered the saddle and side of Days, and he could see that the blood came from his sister, not the horse.

'Larns!' he called as he sprinted. 'Larns! Are you OK?'

Days turned his head towards Dane and nickered softly, his eyes sad in the starlight, and he nudged Lani with his muzzle.

The sand seemed to grab at Dane's feet, slowing him as he strained to run faster. He felt trapped in a dream where he tried to run through mud but got nowhere, and each second dragged out longer than the one before as he tried to reach his sister. He had sat helpless next to his father as he'd died, and his heart was exploding at the thought of repeating that experience with Lani.

Please don't let her be dead, his thoughts ran a million times faster than his legs, *not again, not my sister.*

She opened her eyes and saw her brother running towards her. 'Steady on,' she smiled, 'I'm OK.'

The pain which had been stabbing into Dane's chest lifted instantly. He stopped and bent over, his hands on his knees as he drew huge gulps of air into his lungs. Taking the time to wipe the tears from his face before standing upright, he uttered up a silent thanks for the lives of his brother and sister.

'You had me worried,' he said as he walked the last few steps towards her.

'Did you think the Min Min had come for me?'

'Something like that,' he sank to his heels next to her and looked worriedly at her leg. 'Looks to be a lot of blood. How bad is it?'

'More than a scratch, less than having my leg cut off – pick somewhere between those two, but I'm going to be OK.' Her eyes glowed as she looked at Dane, 'Dad told me so.'

Dane met her eyes and remained silent. He could not think of anything to say. It was clear that Lani believed she had spoken with their father, but he was dead.

'He was here, Dane,' Lani leaned towards him, her expression earnest as she tried to make him believe. 'He was here, and Fleet was with him. I saw them.'

'Saw who?' asked Matthew as Misty stopped next to Days.

'Dad and Fleet. They were with the lights.'

Matthew looked to Dane for a clue as to how to

respond, but Dane only shrugged.

'It's true,' Lani insisted, 'and I can prove it.'

She began to relate her experience to them, keen to share it with her brothers while it was still fresh in her mind.

When she had collapsed, the lights hovered near her. She looked up to see a pair of glowing orbs shedding their light over her, and a sense of gentleness flowed from them, dispelling any fear. The air next to them shimmered as though it was the surface of a pool of water rippled by the wind. She stared, fascinated by the patterns in the air that hinted at something forming from the air itself.

She sensed the presence of her father and was almost prepared to see him before he stepped out of the undulating surface of air in front of her. The transparent air parted, and he formed - her father, dressed in his usual jeans and blue shirt, one hand resting on the neck of Fleet, who stood beside him. Only this was not the older, grey Fleet that had been left lying dead in the dirt. This Fleet was shining with light and had the dark mane and tail of his youth.

'No need to look so surprised, Little Rabbit,' he gave her one of the nicknames he'd called her throughout her childhood. 'I always told you that you'd find me here.'

'Daddy!' she cried, not sure if she was seeing him or having a hallucination due to blood loss. 'And you've got Fleet!'

He chuckled, 'You don't think that I'd leave him once he joined me. He's looked after you for so many years; it's time I looked after him.' He patted the grey neck. Fleet shook his head and looked around alertly.

'Those men, Dad, they shot him, and me, too.'

'I can see,' her father came closer and knelt beside her to look at her leg. 'Nothing vital hit. You'll be fine, just a bit sore for a while, and then you'll have a great scar to go with the story of your camping trip here.'

'We wanted to see the Min Min,' she told him.

A burst of laughter met that statement, 'And it looks as though you got more than you bargained for, eh? It seems the Min Min wanted to see you, too.'

'Dane and Matthew are still back there,' she looked past him to the glow from the Galaxy Walk around the bend of the canyon. 'I don't know if they got away from the men or not. I should have gone back.'

'You did exactly what you should have done,' he told her, 'and don't worry about them – they're going to be fine.'

'Are you sure, or are you just saying that?'

'I *know* they're going to be fine. You all are.' He reached out and patted the top of her head gently. 'You're not going to join me for a long, long time. None of you. Amy's right about all the things you're going to achieve – that's if you are willing to work hard enough for them. Dreams come true with hard work.'

'Are you a dream, Dad?' Lani reached out and took his hand, turning it over in hers. 'Are you really here?' His hand looked real. It felt warm. She held it to her face, rested her cheek on his hand, and closed her eyes, sighing deeply. This *was* her father.

'I am here,' he told her, 'but not for long, not like this. Remember, though, that I'm always here for you, I watch over you on sports day at school, and I'll be there at Christmas. I'll be there on all your important days and whenever you need me. You won't see me as you can tonight, though, but I'll be there. The Min Min let me come through like this so you could see me, and Fleet, too, of course.'

'The Min Min?'

'They're like guardians and guides,' he explained. 'Those old stories about them coming to steal souls are partly right – they come to guide souls over to the other place.'

'Heaven? Are they angels taking you to heaven?'

'I guess you could call it heaven; lots of people do. It's difficult to explain. It's like another universe that exists in the same place as this one, but it's not made of matter like this one. It's made of light and energy.'

'Light is energy,' pointed out Lani, remembering something her science teacher had said.

'So it is. And your soul is energy. So is Fleet's soul and everyone else's. Your body can't ever cross to this universe, but your energy can. And there are places, like here in the gorge, where it's easy for the energy to pass back and forth between these parallel universes.'

'Parallel universes?'

'Google them,' he smiled at her. 'And here, in the gorge, the Min Min can cross over easily, which is why they are sighted so often around here. We always knew this was a special place, though, didn't we?'

Lani nodded. It was why they rarely brought any visitors here, only the most trusted, like Dane and Amy. It was a sacred place.

'You have to make sure you keep it special, though, you understand?' He waited for her to nod again. 'What happens tonight needs to remain a secret.'

'I don't think anyone would believe us, anyway,' she pointed out.

'Someone would, and they'd come here and ruin this place. The Min Min came through to help all of you tonight, and, in return, you need to keep their secret. Can you do that?'

'I can, but what about Dane and Matthew? They're not going to believe that I've spoken to you. I'm not even sure

I am speaking to you.'

'Dane and Matty are easy,' he grinned. 'Tell Matty I know why the rooster died, and he's not to worry. He was due to die anyway - it wasn't his rubber snake on a string that gave him a heart attack. I know he's been worried about that. And tell Dane he doesn't need to keep my jumper under his pillow at school – I'm with him, I'm with all of you. I'm not with my clothes or my grave or tied to any of the things I once owned. He takes it out in the middle of the night and holds it, and he puts his hand up for me to high five, and I always do. He can't feel my hand, but I'm there. Tell them that, and they'll know I've been here tonight.'

'Can you wait until they're here so they can see you too?'

He shook his head, 'They wouldn't be able to see me, Little Rabbit – it's because you've come close to dying that you're able to see Fleet and me. But you're going to be fine. When you wake up, you'll feel better. And it's your job to stay alive for as long as you can, no matter what life throws at you – you can't get here by trying to die, only by trying to live.'

He knew that she would have times of great sadness ahead in her life, and she would wonder how she would get through them, so he needed her to have this message. 'No matter what happens, remember that while there is life, there is hope. I need you to promise me now that you will always choose life – that is the only road to this place where Fleet and I will be waiting for you. Promise me.'

'I promise, Daddy,' she whispered, unaware that in many years when she was so sad that she didn't think she could go on living, that promise would keep her alive.

'Fleet and I have to go, now, but Dane and Matty will be here shortly. You're going to wake up feeling stronger, and Mum will be here before too long. Make sure you tell them that they need to keep some things a secret, but I think they'll work that out for themselves, anyway.'

'Can't you stay, please?' Lani didn't want to see them go, she wanted to keep on looking at Fleet, who looked so beautiful and happy standing there with her father, and she wanted to keep talking to her father. She never wanted him to leave.

'I have to go, sweetie; it's time for you to wake up. But I'll always be with you when you need me.'

Lani thought she heard a horse call out, somewhere far in the distance, and Fleet turned his head away as though he'd heard the call, too.

'That's Flirty calling for him,' her father explained, naming Fleet's dam, a mare that had died several years earlier. 'She knows it's time for us to go back.'

'That's Flirty?' Lani asked, remembering the grey mare from when she was young. 'Do all horses go there?'

'Pretty much,' he gave her one last smile. 'Don't you remember that I always said I'd only go to a place that let in dogs and horses?'

He leaned over to kiss the top of her head, as he used to when she was a little girl, then he and Fleet turned away and disappeared into a shimmering pool of air. A pair of lights floated away into the night sky. Lani opened her eyes to find Dane running towards her, an expression of dread on his face.

CHAPTER FIFTEEN
Keeping Secrets

Lani related the messages from their father, leaving the two key pieces about Matthew and Dane until last. As she told the story of the rooster, Matthew looked alarmed, then relieved. He realized that no one else knew about him teasing his mum's prize rooster that died shortly after, so their father had been there to tell Lani about the incident. Dane listened to the story about him keeping his father's jumper and holding his hand up to the empty air at night to high-five someone who wasn't there, and he narrowed his eyes to force back the tears that threatened to fall. No one knew about that. No one. Except for his father.

'So, do you believe me now?' Lani looked between her two brothers. 'It was Dad. I might have been unconscious, but I'm telling you, Dad was here.'

'Who was?' asked Brandon as he arrived, puffed from his climb down the canyon wall.

'Tell him,' Dane nodded at his sister.

'Dad was here, with Fleet,' she told him, 'but if Amy is going to be here soon, I'll wait, so I don't have to repeat it all a third time if that's OK.'

'She's up there,' Brandon pointed up at the top of the gorge where the last of the fire had diminished to a glow and flashed his torch twice. Two flashes came back immediately. 'She has Nu-man and Shandy there and Blaze. Do you want me to tell her to come down?'

'No, I'll just have to repeat it all a third time,' Lani sighed. 'Amy's better off staying up there with the horses than trying to come down that goat track in the dark – only an idiot would attempt that.'

The flash of white teeth as she smiled removed the barb from her words, and Brandon wasn't in the least offended. She knew how he'd risked his life to come down into the canyon for them. She also knew he wouldn't appreciate a fuss being made over his heroic efforts when a joke would do.

'I would have felt like an idiot if I'd fallen,' he admitted, 'and I don't think Amy should attempt it.'

Dane agreed, 'I think she's safest up there. We don't know what's happened with those men, and I don't want to stay here too long if there's any chance they could come after us.'

'You don't think the Min Min took care of them?' Matthew asked anxiously. He didn't want to meet up with the men again.

'I don't know what the Min Min have done,' Dane glanced back at where the light from the Galaxy Walk was beginning to glow with the moonlight, 'but I think we should keep moving if we can, just in case they come after us. I'm hoping they've been scared halfway back to Brisbane, but I don't want to sit around for too long to find out.'

'Will you be able to ride Days?' Brandon asked Lani, looking at her bloody leg in the beam of his torch. 'Or do you want Dane and me to try and carry you?'

'Given the choice,' she managed a grin, 'I'll always choose the horse. I will need some help getting on, though. This leg doesn't seem to want to move.'

'Do you think it hit bone?' Dane leaned over to help his sister to her feet.

'I hope I never get to say these words again in my life,' she sniffed, 'but I think it's only a flesh wound.'

'I got smashed over the head with a gun,' Matthew gave a quick laugh. 'I hope I never have to say that again, either.' He grabbed at his head and winced. 'Ouch. Laughing hurts – and that's one more thing I don't want to be repeating any time soon.'

'You Winters are tough,' Brandon stepped in to help Dane lift Lani onto Days' back. 'Pistol-whipped and shot, and you're still riding horses.'

'Yup,' said Matthew, 'it'll take more than guns and bullets to stop us from riding.'

After Brandon signaled to Amy to let her know that they were going further into the canyon, he took up a position next to Days so that Lani could tell him about seeing her father and Fleet. He listened quietly without doubting her words, but he thought the vision could have been a product of her blood loss and shock rather than reality.

'No one knows about that,' Dane confirmed when Lani related the proof her father had offered to convince her brothers. 'Don't ask me how or why, but, I'm telling you - there's no way Larns could have made that up.'

'Fair enough,' Brandon accepted Lani's belief. After what he'd seen with his own eyes that night, it made him realize that possibilities were greater than he had ever imagined, but he remained quietly skeptical as that was his nature.

'So, once we get out of all this,' said Dane, 'we probably should keep quiet about the Min Min.'

'That's not a problem with me,' Brandon shook his head. 'If we try and explain what we've seen tonight, most people will think we're nutters and others will come here for a look, and it'll become a tourist attraction for weirdos. I don't want to come here over summer for a swim and try and fight my way through a crowd of crystal hugging crazies here to worship the Min Min.'

'I guess we just tell the police the truth about our part in it,' Dane suggested. 'We used the UFO kites and the fire to create a distraction, and we made a bolt for it. If they catch those men and they go on about all the lights, it'll just look like they are making it up or hallucinating. Agreed?'

The others assented and walked along in silence. The light from the rising moon was creeping down the canyon walls towards them, driving the shadows back so that they could make out their way between the rocks of the narrowing gorge. They all listened for the sounds of the men pursuing, but the canyon remained silent and dark behind them. It seemed the Min Min had departed and the men had gone the other way, or so they hoped. If they heard them following, they had no plans in place apart from trying to outrun them.

'Can we get through the gorge to the other side?' Brandon asked, thinking about how they would escape if the men came after them.

'We can,' Dane replied. 'I'm not sure if the horses will make it through, though.'

'I wish we knew what *they* are doing,' Matthew looked back over his shoulder.

'We will soon,' Brandon reassured him, pointing overhead. 'The moon will be high enough, before long, to shine on the canyon floor, and then our eye in the sky will be able to see where they are. Amy will let us know if they're following.'

He knew Amy was bringing the two horses along the top of the canyon as he'd used his torch to signal her to follow, and she'd replied twice since then, briefly flashing her torch down onto the rocks in front of him to show that she was keeping up.

Amy had no trouble working out what Brandon had meant when he'd shone his torch on himself, pointed at his chest and then down the canyon. He was telling her that they were going further into the gorge. When he pointed at her and motioned along the top of the walls, he meant that she should follow along. Finally, he pointed to her, his eyes, and behind him, meaning that she should watch for the men.

She collected Nu-man and Shandy from where they were tied and led them along the path visible under the light of the full moon. Blaze trotted a few steps ahead of her, winding his way along the track with his senses alert for anything that might threaten them. Once, he stopped and raised his hackles, growling lightly at something ahead, but the subsequent thumping noises indicated a kangaroo or wallaby, and it had been too scared of them to stay where it had been grazing.

Several times she halted as the progress of the ones below was slower, and she did not want to get ahead of them. She tied the horses to a tree and went to the edge of the canyon to look down. It was difficult to see as the canyon was so much darker than on the top of the hills, but she could hear the sounds of hooves below. When she checked behind them, there wasn't any sign of the men following them. There was no sign of the Min Min, either.

It was eerily quiet. As Amy sat near the edge looking down into the shadows of the gorge that split the hills in two, she was glad of Blaze sitting at her side. It seemed as though they were alone in this enormous moonlit landscape of the outback, and yet she was not frightened, merely aware of how small she was in this vastness of land and sky. She felt as though she was a part of it: she belonged here. At first, she had thought that if they could get through this night to daylight, all would be safe. Now she realized that the night was their friend. The protective embrace of the land helped hide from the evil that was those men.

'Come on, boy,' she whispered to the dog as she rose to her feet, sure that no one followed the group below. Blaze looked up at her and wagged his tail.

By the time the moonlight reached the floor of the canyon, she estimated it must have been after ten o'clock, and they had been walking for several hours, but because the group below was moving so slowly and had stopped several times to help Lani off Days and check her leg, they had not even reached the half-way point.

Amy gave a brief whistle to attract their attention and saw all their faces turn her way, pale ovals in the moonlight.

'I'm going further back to check if anyone's following you,' she whispered loudly over the edge, hoping her voice would carry down to them as easily as their voices carried up.

Judging by the thumbs up from Dane and Brandon, they had heard her.

'We'll wait here,' Dane's stage whisper reached her. 'Matty and Larns aren't feeling too sharp.'

'Back soon,' she replied.

Leaving the horses tied up to a tree, she and Blaze jogged back down the track, stopping every hundred meters or so to examine the floor of the canyon for any signs of movement or life. There was none. The gorge appeared to be empty. She went as far back as the Galaxy Walk, its walls once more glowing with light as the moonlight reflected a million times from the crystals in the rock, but there was no sign of the men. They were alone.

She ran fast back to the horses, covering in twenty minutes what had taken hours at a halting walk.

'I think they've gone,' she called out to the group below who sat or lay on the sand at the edge of a narrow pool of water. 'Rest up if you want. I'm going to take the horses and head back to the house.'

It was not too much further to Legend's Leap, and she knew the way from there back to the homestead.

'Good idea,' Dane spoke softly, 'when you get there…'

His voice broke off suddenly, and he pointed to the slash of sky he could see behind them. Amy turned to see lights in the sky. The Min Min were back. As soon as the thought entered her head, it was chased out by the realization that this was one light, not a pair, and the distant throbbing of the helicopter was already reaching her ears.

'Chopper!' Matty cried out.

'Can you signal him?' Dane called to Amy.

'He's too far away, but I'll try, anyway. It looks as though he's heading to our campsite.'

Although they all knew that the helicopter meant help was on its way, they also realized that it would be quite some time before Lani received the medical help she required as it would be impossible to airlift her out of the canyon, she would have to leave the way she came in. Dane made his sister as comfortable as he could as he thought about their next steps.

'I'd say that chopper is the police. Someone must have found our camp and the note and put it all together and called them. The quickest way to get help for Matty and Larns, now, is if someone can reach them and get them to call out for a medivac team. I know Amy will want to get a message to them, but I don't want her to be alone near the camp in case those men are back there now.'

'But you're not worried about them getting me?' Brandon gave his friend a look of dry humor.

'Nah,' Dane chuckled, 'you're as tough as an old goanna – they wouldn't want to try and grab you. Anyway, Amy doesn't know to keep the Min Min a secret, so best if one of us can get there first to give her a heads up on that.'

'I'd better get a move on then. She's going to have a faster path up there than I have. If I run into our friends,' Brandon looked grim, 'I'll ride them down. They ran out of bullets firing at the Min Min, and I'll back a horse against an empty gun any day of the week.'

'Call out if you run into trouble. Take Days. I'll be following with Lani and Matty. They can double up on Misty. With you riding in front, we should have a safe path.'

Brandon looked at Matthew and Lani, both lying on the sand, their eyes closed as they dealt with their pain and tried to rest. His heart was filled with dismay as he looked at their pale skin and knew they needed help as soon as possible.

'I always wanted to have a go on that palomino,' he nodded at the big horse standing near Lani.

'Take care of him,' Lani murmured without opening her eyes.

'I'll try not to break him,' Brandon told her, 'but, you know, someone should teach you to clean up a horse after you've ridden him - he looks an awful mess with all your blood down his side.'

Lani managed a grin at his words, 'That's what grooms are for - find a deep waterhole and swim him through it for me, will you?'

'You know,' chuckled Brandon as he mounted Days, 'I

think you're faking that bullet hole so that you get out of doing your work.'

'It's working,' she muttered back, opening her eyes at last and giving him a look of deep understanding that took them back through all their years of knowing each other. She knew he was worried about her and Matty. He knew she wanted to thank him for being there. Instead, they handled it with jokey words that covered their love for each other without hiding it altogether. She was like the sister he'd never known, and he was like a third brother as well as a good friend.

'Ride safe,' she closed her eyes again.

'Always,' Brandon replied softly.

From above, Amy watched Brandon mount her horse and ride away. 'I'm going, too,' she called down to her cousins, 'No need to fill me in; I heard everything.'

Looking up at her, Dane gave her a thumbs up. 'Keep an eye out for those men, and don't get off your horse until the police or Mum or someone else is there, OK?'

'No problem with that,' she replied.

As Amy mounted Shandy at the top of the canyon wall, leaving Nu-man with the rope wrapped around his neck so that he could follow at will, Dane helped his brother and sister onto Misty and began leading them back down the gorge. Amy had a sense of the tide turning. They had all headed away from camp earlier; now, with the sighting of the helicopter in the distance, they were flowing back towards it. Once more, Blaze led the way, on the alert for any danger, but he didn't pause to growl or even stare at shadows. He loped along in the moonlight with Amy and the horses following.

In the canyon, Brandon was enjoying riding the big palomino as they wove their way back between the rocks which were now clearly outlined by the full moon overhead. He slowed when he reached the Galaxy Walk and looked carefully for any sign of the men, but nothing moved apart from the reflections of the moon's light from the crystals. Assuming they had run for their lives back out the gorge, he continued, though more carefully in case they were waiting in the shadows. In part, he trusted Days' instinct for danger as horses had survived for hundreds of thousands of years by avoiding ambush attacks from predators. While the palomino's ears remained pricked and he continued along calmly, he assumed that no person was hiding behind a rock about to jump out and grab him.

He and Amy rode out of the Sunhaven Hills within minutes of each other, and in the bright light of the moon, he was able to see her waiting at the mouth of the canyon. As he drew alongside her, he noticed that she looked pale in the moonlight, her eyes wide as though startled.

'Are you OK?' he asked.

'I saw something...' she began, then shook her head and blinked.

'The men? Are they here?'

She shook her head again, 'One of them might be around, but two of them...Two of them are gone. They're just gone.'

Brandon narrowed his eyes 'Gone?'

'Gone,' she repeated. 'I can't explain, but I think we only have one to worry about.'

Realizing that she had seen something that distressed her, he changed the subject as they urged the horses into a trot and continued towards the campsite.

'Hey, I can see why you ride tall horses. It's fun looking down on other riders.'

'Poor little Shandy,' she patted the chestnut neck. 'He might not be that tall, but he has a huge heart. And Numan has been a champion, following along calmly.'

'That's my boy,' pride was clear in his voice as he looked at his Quarter Horse.

'Are Lani and Matty going to be OK?' she asked him, expecting the truth with the others out of earshot.

'I think so,' he lifted his shoulders in a shrug. 'Lani has lost a lot of blood, but she still has her sense of humor. Matty has a bit of a headache, and Dane said that Jake bloke kicked him pretty hard while he was down, but it doesn't look like he broke anything.'

'What sort of a mongrel kicks a ten-year-old kid?' Amy's voice held utter disgust. 'I hope they made it back to camp and are caught by whoever is there.'

'Don't forget, if they go on about the Min Min lights, we have to make it clear there weren't any. It was just us with the UFO kites.'

'As far as the Min Min are concerned, my lips are sealed,' she promised. 'They are too powerful to cross, believe me.'

Intrigued by her words but understanding that she didn't want to talk about it, he bit back the questions he was keen to ask. Ahead, the noise of the chopper changed pitched, and it began to descend. They slowed the horses to a walk to watch.

'Looks like the chopper is landing at the campsite,' said Brandon.

'Let's get going, then,' Amy urged the tired Shandy back into a canter and added in a soft voice to her mount. 'I know, boy, but it's nearly over now. When we're back at camp, you can have a big rest and a feed.'

They rode side by side, with Blaze in front and Nu-man a few strides behind. As they neared the campsite, they saw several cars parked there, with the lights of another approaching. The chopper was sitting on the open ground beside the vehicles, its rotor slowing as uniformed men and a woman climbed out. Blaze started to growl at all the activity, but Amy told him to be quiet; these were friends. As the last car pulled up, they could see it was Eleanor Winter and her brother-in-law, John, their expressions of worry and fear clear to see even from a distance.

Everyone looked up as Amy and Brandon cantered into the campsite. Eleanor ran towards them, her face a mix of relief to see them and worry that her children were not with them.

'Thank heavens you are alright!' she exclaimed, pulling Amy into an embrace as she slid off Shandy. 'Where are the others?'

'They're going to be OK,' Brandon rushed to assure her as he stepped off Days and was caught up in Mrs. Winter's loving arms. 'They're coming back down the gorge. Matty and Lani are going to need some help, that's all, but they're going to be fine.'

'Are there three men with them?' A police officer moved forward and questioned him before he could say anything else. 'Are they being held by these men?' He held up photos of Jake, Meat, and Skinner and leaned forward to examine Brandon's reactions.

'They did have Lani, Dane, and Matthew,' he replied slowly and carefully, 'but Amy and I managed to frighten them, and they ran off. They hit Matthew and shot Lani in the leg.'

Mrs. Winter gasped and staggered so that Amy had to step closer to support her.

'They're going to be OK,' he added quickly. 'Dane is bringing them back out of the canyon now, so it'd be good if you could organize someone to help them.'

'And you've just come out of there yourself?' the officer asked, admiring the coolness of both the teens.

'Yes, sir,' Brandon nodded. 'There was no sign of the

men, and nowhere else they could have gone except out here onto the open country.'

The policeman turned to one of the uniformed men beside him and nodded, 'Go back up and look for them; use the infra-red. They should light up like beacons out here. I'll get the lad to take us to the other children. Call for an ambulance to come from Winton.'

Over the next few minutes, the helicopter's noise wound back up to flying level while the officer with Brandon and Amy explained how they had come to be there. Earlier that evening, one of the jackaroos from a station down the road dropped into the campsite after seeing unusual headlights circling there. The mysterious lights flew towards the gorge, and he looked around the camp and found Dane's note.

Realizing that something was seriously wrong because Dane mentioned both parents when everyone knew Geoff Winter was dead, he radioed through to his station on his car's two-way and had them call the police. With the search for the three men focussed on the outback routes through to the Territory, there were response teams within hours of Sunhaven, and they converged on the hills. These were merely the first to arrive. A full-scale search involving hundreds of police would be underway by morning if they had not captured the three escapees before then.

'The neighbors rang me at March's place,' Mrs. Winter told them, 'and John was already on his way back because the Winton police gave him the heads up at the meeting about the problems here.'

'If you're right to go, son,' the officer looked at Brandon, 'you can guide us back to your friends. You'll be safe with us.'

Amy gave Brandon a wry smile. They had done alright for themselves without police protection, she thought, but the men seemed to assume they were frightened teenagers who needed reassurance. She cringed at the thought of the counseling that would be offered to them after this night as adults tried to help them through the trauma of the events. All they would want to do is ride their horses and get over it. Then she bit back a giggle at the thought of the psychologists, psychiatrists, and counselors who would be involved if they spoke of the role the Min Min played in the night's drama.

'Can you ride?' Brandon asked the three officers standing near him, waiting to go into the canyon.

They shook their heads. 'We'll take the four-wheel-drive,' one pointed at a police vehicle

'Won't do you much good once we reach the canyon,' Brandon advised. 'If you don't mind, I'll take a horse, and when we get there, you can follow on foot. I don't want to walk if I can help it.'

'That works with us,' the head officer told him.

'If you're right with Shandy and Nu-man,' Brandon spoke to Amy, 'I'll take Days for another spin as he's already saddled, and I don't feel like going bareback again.'

'Go for it. I'm glad you like riding him.'

'He's not bad for a big yella fella,' he patted the palomino neck. 'Looks like you're going to be safe here. We should be back before too long.'

'You need something to eat and drink before you go back out,' Mrs. Winter fussed over Brandon. 'You must be starving.'

'I have that covered,' said John Winter, handing Brandon a sandwich and a sports drink that he'd fetched from his vehicle. 'I bought these earlier tonight. They were going to be my dinner, but my plans have changed a bit since then.'

They had been running on adrenalin since the afternoon

and hadn't realized they were ravenous until they saw the food. Brandon took the offerings with thanks and mounted Days, guiding him back towards the gorge as the police followed in their vehicle. Mrs. Winter told Amy she would organize something for her to eat and headed to the gooseneck. Uncle John offered to put the horses away, but Amy insisted that she bed the horses down for the night and feed and water them herself.

'I'll follow along then,' he told her. 'I'll give you some time to yourself, but I'll be close by if you need me.'

'I think those men will be long gone,' she informed him. She knew that two of them would never be coming back. 'They had a pretty big fright from the UFO kites and the fire, and I don't think they'll be coming anywhere near lights for a while.'

'And the real Min Min?' he asked her, his brows raised.

'Are we even sure they exist?' she countered.

'I heard that jackaroo say he saw headlights near the camp tonight and saw them moving back towards the gorge. Now, you and I both know, they weren't *headlights* he was seeing.'

'It makes you wonder, doesn't it?' She gave him a speculative look as though she was considering the possibility that the Min Min had made an appearance that night. 'Maybe the others will have something to say about it. I think we're pretty safe here from those men at the moment, though.'

'You don't think they are going to come here and turn themselves over to the police?'

'I think they'll be out in the downs running like rabbits, away from the police and away from any lights.'

He chuckled at her evasion, guessing that she was hiding a good Min Min story. He hoped he would hear it once a few days had passed and the police were out of the scene. For now, he would stay near Amy as she settled the horses down for the night in case she was wrong about the men avoiding the epicenter of police action. He would remain far enough away to allow her some space with the horses but close enough to help if danger appeared out of the night.

The quiet minutes alone with the horses were a breath of heaven, and, as she led them to their yards, she leaned against Shandy's neck and pressed her cheek to his chestnut hide, thankful that the events were coming to an end. She did not think she would ever be able to describe what she had seen in the minute she had waited for Brandon at the mouth of the canyon. She wasn't even sure what she had seen.

With the police, Uncle John, and Aunt Eleanor nearby, she felt safe. The police would capture the remaining one who had run from the Min Min. Looking back at the lights of the campsite, the cars, the activity, the helicopter beating its way through the air to search for the men, she felt a huge sense of relief. In the distance, she could see Brandon on Days lit by the car's headlights as he led the police to the canyon, and she smiled. He sure could ride.

Blaze growled at the shadows near the horse yards under the gidyea trees. He moved to stand in front of Amy, his hackles up for a few seconds before bursting into ferocious barking. Shandy and Nu-man snorted and pulled back, yanking on Amy's arms, as the figure of Skinner erupted out of the gloom, his teeth bared in a manic grin. He threw himself at the girl with the horses, his body colliding with her before she could react. He knocked the wind from her as they went down in the dirt.

He pinned her down with his weight and held his hand over her mouth to stop her from calling out for help, ignoring the frenzied biting of the kelpie that savaged his legs and arms, drawing blood with every bite.

An insane light burned in his eyes, and he muttered over and over, 'The dust. All dust. Dust to dust, dust to dust.'

A vile cackling sound emerged in his throat. It could have been laughter or may have been a human version of growling.

He mistook Amy for Lani and believed this was the girl who had led him into that valley of demons, and he wanted to punish her for what had happened. The tearing teeth of the dog were not worrying him as he was past feeling pain. His experience of meeting the Min Min was beyond anything that the children could imagine. The terror of what they'd shown him had driven him insane.

John Winter reached the pair on the ground within seconds. He grabbed Skinner by the back of the neck and hauled him backward, driving a fist into the side of his head to make him release Amy. A normal man would have been knocked unconscious by the blow, but Skinner has passed any normal limits, and he turned his crazed eyes on John, letting Amy go so that he could launch himself at his assailant. A second blow landed on Skinner's jaw, but he shook his head like a bull and drove both fists at John in a lightning-fast combination learned from many years in jail. His sanity may have gone, but his instinct to fight remained.

Although he tried to defend himself from the punches, John had no hope of stopping the demented attack. His head snapped back as blow after blow hit him in the face. Blaze continued sinking his teeth into Skinner's legs as John collapsed to the ground, knocked out by one of the fists to his jaw.

The escapee turned his violence against the dog. Driving a vicious kick into the kelpie, he sent him flying through the air. Amy cried his name as she saw her loyal friend hit a tree trunk. Blaze did not respond. He lay where he fell, silent and unmoving.

Satisfied that he'd rid himself of the man and dog, Skinner came back to stand over Amy who was trying to crawl away from him. He laughed at her attempt to flee and drew a knife out of the sheath strapped to his leg and held it up to the moonlight so that he could admire the lethal lines of the narrow blade before he used it to kill the girl. With the knife in front of him ready to slice into Amy, he stepped forward to kill her, his eyes burning with murderous fever.

He didn't see the palomino coming at full gallop. He didn't look up to see Brandon swinging the steel stirrup around on the end of the stirrup leather. He wasn't aware of it driving into his temple and knocking him off his feet. The last conscious thought was looking forward to destroying the girl in front of him, then blackness fell.

When Blaze had first barked, Brandon recognized the tone. He knew it wasn't a mild warning bark or the sound of a dog yapping at shadows: Amy was in danger, and Blaze was ready to die for her. Without hesitating, he wheeled Days around and jabbed his heels into his sides, lifting the horse into a gallop. He could see the vague outlines of the horses near the yards and could make out the figures of people, but it was the fierce sounds coming from Blaze that alerted him to the full menace of what was happening in the shadows of the gidyea trees.

As he galloped, he took his right foot out of the stirrup and wrenched the stirrup leather back so that it came off the saddle. He began swinging the stirrup around as he rode, knowing what an effective weapon it could be when used like this. When he was close enough, he could make out John on the ground with Skinner standing over Amy, his arm raised with a knife that was about to be plunged into her. In the last instant, he saw Amy's head turn as she realized he was there, and their eyes locked for the tiniest instant that would last the rest of their lives. He struck Skinner in the head with the full force of a swing, sending the man reeling, aware he may well have killed him but not caring.

Days skidded to a halt, and he threw himself off and ran to Amy, who was leaning over John. She gave him the warmest of looks, thanking him with her eyes as they helped John sit up. Eleanor and two policemen arrived at a run, quickly checking that they were unhurt before turning their attention to John and leaving them to tend to Blaze, who was now standing over Skinner's unconscious form, growling softly at him.

'Looks like he had a good chew,' Brandon nudged the bloodied legs with his foot. 'Good dog.'

'Bet he tasted awful,' Amy wrinkled her nose. She wanted to find the right words to let Brandon know what she felt at this moment, but as he stood beside her, looking down at her, she could only look into his eyes and leave the words unsaid.

'Do you think I killed him?' he asked, unable to verbalize the emotions that he was feeling - that he had felt when he saw Skinner poised, knife in hand, ready to strike her.

'Nah,' she shook her head, 'his chest is still going up and down. Would you have felt bad if you'd killed him?'

'Not if it meant saving you.'

HORSES OF THE LIGHT

CHAPTER SIXTEEN
Jake and Meat

Before attacking Amy, Skinner ran from the lights that gathered around him. He ran from the horrendous images of his life that played back to him. All the misery and pain that he had inflicted on others came back to him and, in a blinding agony of enlightenment, he understood that this is what he had chosen for his life. He screamed and clawed away from the lights that swirled around him and stumbled from the vileness that came from his choices.

He looked back to see Meat and Jake held by the lights, their arms raised, their faces contorted in agony as they were shown their lives. *You always had the choice*, a voice whispered inside their heads, *and these were the choices you made.* Their mouths were open in screams that made no sound. Their eyes stared at what they had brought to the lives around them.

Falling, then crawling backwards through the sand, Skinner pushed himself further away from the terror of the lights. He could not take his eyes off his companions, pinned like insects in a display case. The air seemed to unzip in front of them, revealing a brightness of laser intensity that cut towards the two figures. For a few seconds, the brilliance of the light hurt Skinner's eyes, but he could not turn away.

It cut into Meat and Jake, the glare enveloping them and raising them off the ground. They hung in the air, surrounded by a light so powerful that it looked as though a piece of the sun had dropped into the canyon. For a few seconds, they were able to scream, and the sounds coming from them spoke of unbearable agony. In those seconds, all the pain they had given to others through their lives came back at them. Their bodies seemed to vibrate and then dissolve, disappearing into a billion fragments of dust that clouded the air and swirled. Dust that had no form. There were no bodies, no clothes, no sign of anything except dust that settled on the sand and wafted towards Skinner, touching his skin and sending tendrils into his lungs as he breathed.

At that point, Skinner began screaming again. *Dust to dust*, the funereal words played over and over in his mind as he saw what Meat and Jake had become. Nothing. They had become nothing. They had made their choices, and their life had led to this. Nothing. Dust.

Choking on the dust that entered his lungs, he ran. The sights and sounds of the Min Min had driven sanity from his mind, and he ran without thought, just a desperate need to flee the death that had claimed the other two.

As he fled from the drifting cloud of dust, the lights departed, blinking out of the air of the canyon as they made their way to the other place. As the last of the Min Min left, they called to Geoff Winter and Fleet to follow. The night was over for them. It was time to go home.

CHAPTER SEVENTEEN
Christmas

The police took Skinner into custody and continued to search for Jake and Meat, but they had vanished. Over the next twenty-four hours, the command center at the camping site grew to over fifty police, two helicopters, search equipment, and dogs. The dogs followed the criminals' scent into the gorge, but before reaching the Galaxy Walk, they began howling and refused to go further. The police searched the entire gorge from end to end, from above and on foot, and found no sign of the two men.

The days were cloudy, so they didn't experience the incredible sight of the crystals lighting up in the sunshine. To the searchers, it was quite unremarkable. After a few days, they left the gorge and focused on the surrounding land and homesteads. The men had disappeared. Jake didn't contact his sister. They didn't phone any friends or family. The police thought it was as though they ceased to exist.

Matthew spent a day and a night in the hospital. Lani was there for two days before they were sent home to recuperate. The police advised counseling, but the teens and Matty convinced Eleanor Winter that they would be fine without it. Police questioned them about the events at the campsite and in the gorge. They all had the same story about the cry of the curlew, the UFO kites, and the fire on top of the gorge scaring the men so badly that they ran, and they didn't see them again. It was a simple and almost believable story.

John Winter managed to get the true story out of them after five days. He did not seem the least surprised to hear that his brother Geoff had appeared to Lani and had shown her that he was taking care of Fleet. He and Geoff had grown up roaming the gorge and knew that strange things happened there. They had always half-believed the family stories of the Galaxy Walk being the gateway to heaven. They promised their parents and grandparents to uphold the family tradition of protecting the gorge from outsiders, and he was proud that the children convinced everyone that the bird, kites, and fire were solely responsible for sending Skinner insane and causing the other two to vanish.

By the time Christmas Day rolled around, the police had left, following up possible sightings of Meat and Jake around the state. The bruises on Matthew's face and stomach were a vibrant array of purples and reds with some fading orange at the edges, and he was proud to show everyone and tell them that he had been pistol-whipped and kicked by a thug. Brandon had gone home immediately after the night of the Min Min but had come back to spend Christmas Eve and Christmas Day with the Winters. The counselors accepted that the teens would not speak to them, but they recommended that they spend as much time together as possible to overcome the traumatic experience. Brandon's parents were happy to have him stay over at Sunhaven.

Most days since the camping trip, Amy managed to find some hours to edit the videos they had taken before the criminals arrived. She laughed at the antics of Matthew on the computer screen as she pieced the clips together. When completed, she uploaded five different videos to YouTube and shared the links on Facebook. She hoped the rest of the world would find them as funny as she did. Even after viewing them dozens of times, she laughed. She would show the others after Christmas, perhaps in the New Year when the number of views had climbed past a hundred or so.

Dane and Amy found some time to work their horses each day, usually in the early morning before the heat of the day bared its teeth, but they were quiet about it as Matthew was still too sore to ride, and Lani remained immensely sad over the loss of Fleet. Even though she believed he was in the care of her father, it hurt her deeply to hobble on crutches over to the stables and see his empty stall. She could often be found there, leaning over his door gazing at the space where her grey horse had once stood, wishing his soft eyes were still there to look at her, wishing she could hear his friendly nicker. She knew there were dozens of horses on Sunhaven that she could take over as her new horse, but she had not been ready to say goodbye to Fleet.

On Christmas Eve, instead of going over to the traditional Christmas party at Mahalia's station, the neighborhood came to Sunhaven for carol singing and dinner. Their friends, including Mahalia, listened in rapt admiration as the boys retold the edited story of the afternoon and night at Sunhaven Gorge. Lani and Amy sat shoulder to shoulder, smiling at the antics of the boys as they glossed over the real events with their amusing versions. At the singing of Silent Night under the stars in the garden, Lani's eyes began to fill with tears, so she moved away from the crowd and stared out over the downs hoping to see lights or a sign of her father or Fleet. She didn't notice when Amy came to stand quietly beside her.

'Before my dad went away the last time,' Amy said quietly, 'he told me that he believed everything had a reason, though we weren't always able to understand what that reason was. Sometimes, if something seemed bad, it was because we needed to be somewhere else in life or needed to move on to something else. Sometimes a door had to slam shut before we could open the next one.'

Lani considered her words for a while before asking, 'Do you think I saw Dad and Fleet that night?'

With a light shrug, Amy looked heavenwards at the stars, burning so brilliantly that night before Christmas, 'I know we can't understand everything that goes on around us. I wish I'd seen my dad there that night. I don't even know if he's dead. They just said that he was.'

'It was Dad,' Lani nodded adamantly. 'I don't want ever to doubt what I saw and what he said but, Amy,' she turned to her cousin, tears streaming down her face, falling like diamonds in the night, 'I feel so sad. It's like there's a big weight sitting on my heart pressing down on me, and I can't get rid of it. Every Christmas morning, I get up early and run down to the stables to give Fleet some carrots for his present. Dad used to be there before me, spending time with the horses before we all get up. Fleet was always there for me. Dad, too. But not tomorrow.'

Putting an arm around her cousin's shoulders, Amy found tears running down her cheeks as she felt Lani's pain, 'There are some goodbyes that we'll never be ready for.'

For several minutes they stood together, lost in their thoughts. They went back to join the others, putting on happy faces for the benefit of everyone else.

They went to bed after midnight with reminders from Mrs. Winter that Santa would not arrive while they were awake. When she saw Brandon's smirk she, admonished him with twinkling eyes, 'Brandon Suffolk, don't look so smug. In this house, there are two sorts of people: those who believe in Santa Claus and they are the ones who get presents from Santa, and those who don't believe in him, and they don't get presents from him. Which are you?'

'In that case, I believe in Santa, Mrs. Double-you,' he grinned at her and pulled the sheet up to his nose, 'but that guy in the red suit better have something under the tree for me in the morning, or I'll stop believing.'

'He will,' she assured him and shut the door on the boys' room.

Although Matthew had his own room, he had chosen to sleep in one of the bunks in Dane's room since the episode with the escaped criminals. It seemed to be a sensible arrangement that allowed him to sleep feeling safe. She smiled as she walked away from the door, hearing muffled sounds on the other side. It was good to hear them enjoying some laughs on Christmas Eve.

The girls decided to share a room for a while, as well, though there was no laughter coming from their beds. Eleanor felt helpless in the face of her daughter's sadness. She had offered her the choice of any horse on Sunhaven.

Lani said she would choose a horse in a week or two when she felt better. In the last few days, she had changed the presents from show gear for Fleet to gifts that had nothing to do with the grey horse, and she hoped that she would see some smiles in the morning. Her last thoughts as she went to sleep that night were for her daughter. She wished her husband was there to help her through this.

'Can't you at least wait until sunrise?' Eleanor Winter murmured sleepily as Matthew sat down on the edge of her bed the next morning.

'It is sunrise,' he grinned at her. 'Well, it is somewhere. Maybe between here and New Zealand, the sun is up and shining.'

'Go back to bed,' she rolled over and pulled the sheet up over her head. 'You know the rules about Christmas morning. If you want to get up early, you can have what's in your Santa Sacks and let us sleep until the sun is up.' She uttered the 'we' without thinking. Sometimes it was so easy to forget that Geoff was gone from this place.

'Aw, come on, Mum,' he wheedled, wriggling like an excited puppy. 'We're all awake, and we want you to check what Santa brought you.'

Seeing his bright eyes filled with the excitement of Christmas morning and catching a whiff of freshly brewed coffee wafting from the kitchen, she relented and decided to join them. When she entered the lounge room, she found the five children sitting around the big red pillowcases with their names on them. Their faces turned towards her expectantly.

'We wanted to do this together,' Amy smiled at her aunt as she patted Blaze, who was sitting beside her, 'and that included you. Lani made you coffee.'

A cup of coffee, made just the way she liked it, was

waiting for her on the table, along with a plate of croissants. It was a perfect start to the day, she thought, breakfast and the five best children in the world.

They dug into the Santa Sacks once Eleanor sat with them, drinking her coffee, admiring everything that appeared from the pillowcases, and laughing at their comments. There was the usual assortment of lollies, chocolates, and sugary foods, as well as some games and fun items that had them giggling as they tried on masks and novelty glasses. Eleanor had her own pillowcase with various items in it, mainly practical items that she needed in the kitchen or bathroom.

'Gee, Mum,' Matthew gave the hand creams, towels, and cookbooks a wry look, 'anyone would reckon that you took Santa shopping and got him to buy the sensible things you needed around the house.'

'You would think that, wouldn't you?' she flashed him an amused smile.

'Can we open the main presents now?' he eyed the piles of colorfully wrapped presents under the tree.

'We're all up, so I can't see any reason to wait,' Eleanor spoke the words that released the present opening frenzy.

Matthew dove under the tree and started reading names off the gift tags and handing the presents around, 'Here's one for Dane from Amy, and one for Mum from me. Here, Brandon, this one is from me.'

While Matthew tore the paper off his presents with total abandon, leaving strips of paper all around him, Lani and Amy carefully removed the paper after admiring the wrapping and folded it to one side. Various cries of 'Wow!', 'I love this!' and 'Just what I wanted!' greeted each present. The girls slipped the jewelry on their wrists, they all tried on new t-shirts, and exclaimed over movie and music

DVDs, admired the gifts the others were receiving, and spent the first hour of the day immersed in the joy of giving and receiving.

'Has anyone seen my gift for Lani?' Amy looked around under the tree.

She met Brandon's eyes and raised her brows. He winked at her, and she blushed as she often did when he looked at her that way.

'I think you left it in the car,' he said, 'I'll have a look.'

He had been gone for a couple of minutes when Amy exclaimed, 'No, here it is!'

She handed Lani a small thin present beautifully wrapped in gold and silver paper, but it was no thicker than a few sheets of paper.

'A certificate of appreciation for the world's greatest cousin?' Lani made one of the obligatory guesses about the gift's contents before opening it, turning it over in her hands as she examined it. 'A signed portrait of my favorite band in the world, Gotta B Dreamin?'

'Wrong and wrong,' Amy grinned at her, 'open it and see.'

Sensing that the piece of paper was important, Eleanor stood watching her daughter remove the paper to reveal the registration papers of First Days.

Lani held them in her hand and stared at Amy, her eyes wide with amazement, her hand going to her mouth as her eyes filled with tears. She knew what this meant, and she was overwhelmed.

'They're signed over to you, but you have to fill in your part before you can have him registered in your name with the associations,' Amy told her. 'It's dated today, so he's officially yours now.'

Lani's hand covering her mouth began to quiver, and

she blinked back tears, 'I'm not crying,' she assured her cousin, her voice betraying her emotion. 'I'm so happy. I can't believe it.' The tears fell, and she sniffed and laughed, her eyes bright with joy. 'Well, I *am* crying, but they're happy tears.'

'There he is,' Amy pointed out the window where Brandon held the palomino gelding in the garden, a silver and gold bow tied around the horse's neck shining in the first rays of the sun. 'He's all yours.'

Before grabbing up her crutches and going out to see her new horse, Lani threw herself at her cousin and hugged her tightly. 'I can't believe you've done this,' she gave her a mild shake, 'but I'm not going to give him back as I love that horse, you know I do. I can't believe he's going to be mine!'

'Not *going to be*, he is yours. I think he's going to like show jumping with you.'

As Lani raced out the door as fast as she could on the crutches, Eleanor Winter wiped the moisture from her cheeks and took her niece up in her arms. 'That is the best gift anyone could possibly give,' she told her softly, silently blessing this act of generosity that had lifted the spirits of her daughter. 'I can never thank you enough. I know how much you love him.'

'It was the right thing to do,' Amy replied with a small shrug. 'Anyway, I'll be too busy with Laddie and Jack to ride Days as much as he needs, and I think he was born to be Lani's horse.'

They all followed Lani out to the garden where she had thrown her crutches down and was hanging off Days' neck, her face buried into his mane as she breathed him in. Placing his lead over her arm, Brandon quietly stepped away. He turned towards Amy and smiled, his deep blue eyes crinkling at the edges as they met her green eyes. It was a look of such approval and admiration that Amy found herself catching her breath and hoping he did not share that look with all the other girls who won his smile.

'Did you know about this?' Lani stood on one leg, leaning an arm over Days' neck and using him to balance herself as she looked at her mother.

'I didn't have the faintest inkling of what was going on,' Eleanor replied, 'Did you, boys?'

Both Dane and Matthew shook their heads, 'News to us.'

'I knew,' Brandon admitted, 'but I swore an oath of secrecy.'

'Can I ride, Mum?' Lani looked at her mother with pleading eyes. 'I know I'm not supposed to ride for another week, but I'll be fine… honestly. Walking isn't easy, but sitting on a horse will be OK. Please, please, please.'

Pretending she was about to deny the request, Eleanor shook her head thoughtfully and then smiled, 'Just be careful. Use a mounting block, and don't tire yourself out. A quick ride, mind you, don't head off into the hills. You'd all better go to keep an eye on her.'

Amy ran to find her cousin's helmet then legged her up onto Days, turning the lead rope into a set of reins. With Lani trotting along bareback on Days and Blaze running in circles around them all, they went to the stables to catch their horses. Amy lent Jack to Brandon as he hadn't brought any of his horses over with him for Christmas, and she put a bridle on Laddie.

The sun was climbing quickly, and they didn't want to go far from the house, just a few hundred meters out so that Lani could have the chance to ride Days and they could all be together on horseback for the first time since their camping trip. As usual, Matthew played the clown, enjoying being out on Shandy and his jokes had them all laughing as they walked the horses down the dusty road.

'So, any more camping trips?' Brandon asked his friends, a lopsided grin indicating that he was sure the answer would be negative.

'Not these holidays,' Dane shook his head, 'and I don't know if I want to go up the gorge for a while either. If no one else minds, we might stick to riding out here on the open country and around the house.'

'And making our Min Min videos and putting them on YouTube,' put in Matthew.

'Already done,' Amy confessed. 'I was going to leave it a while before I showed you, maybe when we had a few hundred views, but it seems like they're popular.'

'How popular?' asked Matthew, hoping to have his fifteen minutes of fame.

'I had a quick look this morning.' Amy hesitated before surprising them. 'We have over half a million views, and it's climbing madly. The Min Min are safe as the videos are about us, we don't identify the gorge, and it's not like we're saying there are supernatural beings. But we could make some money out of this.'

'Then I vote we do some more,' said Matthew. 'I think we can spend some time around home getting some more classic moments from me. And I think we're safe in the house doing that.'

'Do we always want to be safe?' Brandon asked, a twinkle in his eyes.

'Safer than having murderers point guns at us would be good,' Matthew replied with a droll expression.

'I'll give you that,' Brandon conceded. 'Still, you have to admit, you are going to march that story out like a pony on parade for the rest of your life, aren't you?'

'Maybe,' Matthew tilted his head to the side, 'unless something more exciting comes along.'

'Not these holidays,' Dane repeated with conviction. 'I vote we just take it easy, work our horses, swim in the creek, and if we hear of any more escaped criminals, we stay in the house.'

'Are you sure those other two can't come back?' Lani looked at Amy closely.

Amy had never clearly explained what she'd seen that night. She had just told them that two of the men had gone and would not come back. The look on her face had warned them that she did not want to discuss what she'd seen that night.

'Did the Min Min take them?' Matthew asked, 'We need to know, Amy – what if they turn up again?'

'They won't turn up anywhere,' Amy told them with quiet conviction, remembering how they had dissolved into dust and blown away.

'Tell us another day,' Brandon could tell from her eyes that the memory distressed her. 'If Amy says they're not coming back, then they're not coming back. They went into the gorge, they didn't go out, and they're not in there anymore, so maybe there are some things that we don't need to know.'

'They won't bother anyone,' Amy assured them a second time and changed the subject, 'so I'm going to spend a lot of time getting Laddie trained.'

'Sounds good to me,' Dane grinned at her, remembering how he'd accused the same plan of being boring when they'd sat on the bus deciding what to do over their holidays. 'Training horses seems a whole lot more fun these days.'

'I am going to start jumping Days,' Lani leaned over and patted his golden neck, 'as long as you are absolutely, positively, completely, and totally sure that you are OK about giving him to me because I'm happy just to borrow him now and then.'

'He's yours,' Amy assured her. 'Don't worry, I thought long and hard about it, so there's no going back. I know this is what I want. You and Days belong together.'

'You know this is the best present I am ever going to get, ever, don't you?'

Amy laughed, 'And this is the best Christmas I've ever had.'

Smiling at her cousin's radiant face, Amy realized that she had never been happier than at this moment: surrounded by family, with Brandon nearby, on her dream horse with a loyal dog on the ground looking up at her. The warmth of giving glowed within, and she felt completely sure that giving Days to Lani was one of the best decisions she would make all her life.

Brandon raised his hand to salute the sun, 'To the Outback Riders.'

'May we take on the world and win,' said Lani, raising her hand like Brandon.

'And can we all grow old together,' Matthew looked from one to the other before adding his hand to those raised.

'And never forget that this is our home,' said Dane, stretching his hand up to the sun.

'We're the Outback Riders,' Amy smiled at her cousins and Brandon, losing her thoughts for a second as his eyes met hers. 'And the outback is our home. We will grow old together, and we will take on the world and win. All of us.'

HORSES OF THE LIGHT

ABOUT THE AUTHOR

Leanne Owens is an English teacher with a Master's in Education who has spent most of her life around horses. She spent many years on sheep and cattle stations in outback Queensland, and combines her knowledge of the outback, horses, and teenagers in The Outback Riders series. Leanne breeds, shows, and trains horses, and has won scores of national and state titles with her Quarter Horses. Currently, she and her husband live on a farm in the south-east corner of Queensland, where she continues to teach, write, and breed horses.

Other books by Leanne Owens:
Horses of the Sun (Outback Riders 1)
Horses of the Fire (Outback Riders 3)
Horses of the Rain (Outback Riders 4)
Horses of the Spirit (Outback Riders 5)

For readers 16 and older:
The Dimity Horse Mysteries
    Book 1 – Muted
    Book 2 – Rescued: Saving the Lost Horses
Flame the Fire Horse and Other Horse Stories
Star Writer – Finding Love Outside Her Books
Zo – She Loved Him for 500 Years

Made in United States
North Haven, CT
22 February 2024